LIFE ON HOMICIDE

LIFE ON HOMICIDE

A POLICE DETECTIVE'S MEMOIR

WILLIAM McCORMACK with BOB COOPER

TORONTO · NEW YORK

Published in 1998 by Stoddart Publishing Co. Limited
34 Lesmill Road, Toronto, Canada M3B 2T6
180 Varick Street, 9th Floor, New York, New York, USA 10014

ORDERING INFORMATION

Distributed in Canada by General Distribution Services Limited
34 Lesmill Road, Toronto, Canada M3B 2T6
Toll-free tel. for Ontario and Quebec 1-800-387-0141
Toll-free tel. for all other provinces and territories 1-800-287-0172
Fax (416) 445-5967
Email Customer.Service@ccmailgw.genpub.com

Distributed in the US by General Distribution Services Inc.
85 River Rock Drive, Suite 202, Buffalo, New York, USA 14207
Toll-free tel. 1-800-805-1083 Toll-free fax 1-800-481-6207
Email gdsinc@genpub.com

02 01 00 99 98 1 2 3 4 5

Cataloging in Publication Data

McCormack, William, 1933–
Life on homicide: a police detective's memoir

ISBN 0-7737-3072-9

1. McCormack, William, 1933– 2. Murder – Ontario – Toronto – Investigation.
3. Murder – Ontario – Toronto. I. Cooper, Bob. II. Title.

HV6535.C33T67 1998   363.25'9523'092   97-932741-5

Photo credits: Russell Rogers, copyright 1978, *The Toronto Star*; Daniel Pearce, copyright 1977, *The Toronto Sun*, a division of Sun Media Corporation. All other photos used with permission of the Metropolitan Toronto Police Services Board.

Jacket design: Bill Douglas @ The Bang
Text design: Tannice Goddard
Computer graphics: Mary Bowness

Printed and bound in Canada

We gratefully acknowledge the Canada Council for the Arts and the Ontario Arts Council for their support of our publishing program.

To the men and women of the Metropolitan Toronto Police and police officers everywhere for their dedication in serving and protecting the public, and to the civilian members of the Force.

Contents

Acknowledgements

First and foremost, I want to express my deep gratitude to William and Margaret McCormack, my parents and the bedrock of my life, and to Jean, my wife, my love, my counsel, and my confidante. To all five of my children – Bill, Kathy, Michael, James, and Lisa – thanks for your love, support, and understanding during my ten years in the Homicide Squad.

I would also like to give special thanks to Staff Superintendent Jack McBride (ret.), Staff Superintendent George Thompson (ret.), Staff Superintendent Jack Webster (ret.), Staff Inspector George Sellar (dec.), Staff Inspector Wayne Smith (ret.), Inspector Herman Lowe (dec.), Sergeant Donald Madigan (ret.), Superintendent Doug Monteath (ret.), and Staff Sergeant Robert E. Cooper (ret.).

To longtime friend and impresario Bill Belfontaine, who encouraged me – no, harrassed me – to write this book, and researcher/writer Bob Cooper, who drew these tales out of me and trimmed my prose down to size, thank you.

Thanks also to my publisher, Jack Stoddart, and to the excellent

ACKNOWLEDGEMENTS

editorial team of Don Bastian, Anne Holloway, and Marnie Kramarich.

I wish also to acknowledge the media of Metropolitan Toronto and the excellent people responsible for the administration of justice in Ontario, some of whom I want to note personally: Brian Greenspan, Q.C., Edward Greenspan, Q.C., Robert McGee, Q.C., Norman Matusiak, Q.C., Peter Shoniker, and the late Mr. Justice Edson Haines.

Prologue

Inspector George Sellar was a brilliant criminal investigator, an inspired leader of men, and the first commander I ever worked for on the Metropolitan Toronto Police Homicide Squad. The first morning I set foot in his office, in the summer of 1969, he gave me a stern warning, which I now pass on to anyone who might have swallowed Hollywood's glamorous image of homicide cops.

"Bill, you're coming into a demanding and highly specialized unit that is unlike any you've ever worked in before, or ever will again, in your police career. And you will find that wherever you go, people are infatuated with the mystique they believe surrounds homicide. But I warn you that although investigation is shrouded in an aura of romanticism, it is one of the dirtiest, foulest, and most disgusting hands-on jobs a person can do. Corpses crawling with maggots. The stench of rotting flesh that stays with you for days. Streets and buildings you can no longer pass without remembering the horrors you've seen there. Victims who remind you of friends and loved ones. If you have a weak stomach or are incapable of separating your personal life from your professional life, don't even attempt it!"

I did attempt it, and during the ten years I was in the squad, from 1969 to 1979, I investigated more than one hundred homicides.

Of course, Sellar was right. Homicide investigation proved to be unlike anything else I had done up to that point in my police career, which began, after growing up in Mauritius, with a delightful five-year stint in Bermuda. There I met and married Jean Kernick, who was raised in Toronto, and who had come to the island for a vacation and decided to stay on and work. When my five-year contract was up, Jean and I decided to move to her home town where I would apply to the city force.

My introduction to Toronto's municipal police force in 1959 was anything but auspicious. I presented myself, along with three other applicants, to the civilian supervisor in charge of the King Street recruitment office. Each of us was handed an application on which appeared many questions, including one about religious affiliation.

After the forms were handed in and several minutes had passed, the supervisor emerged from his office and shook the hands of each of the other three applicants before turning to me and saying, in his thick Scottish brogue, "McCormack, yeh won't do."

"I beg your pardon, sir?"

"I said, yeh won't do. We kenna use yeh."

I was thunderstruck, having learned, as the four of us were waiting for the man to return, that I was the *only* candidate with police experience. I couldn't believe I was being given the cold shoulder without even so much as a reason. Worse still, here I was a young married man, the father of a six-week-old baby, in a strange country with only sixty dollars to my name. What on earth was I going to do? What was I going to tell Jean?

I left the recruitment office and wandered in a daze along the street until I found a small restaurant, where I had a cup of coffee and a cig-arette while I tried to figure out a plan. Then I got mad. I knew there was more than oatmeal stuck in that supervisor's craw. I hailed a taxi and directed the driver to take me to police headquarters, although its location was then still a mystery to me. Somehow, I managed to get in to see Deputy Chief James Dunn, a gentleman if ever there was one. He invited me into his office and had his secretary furnish both of us with coffee, which we sipped as he read my curriculum vitae. When he'd finished reading, he smiled and slid the CV back across the desk to me.

"It seems the supervisor at our recruitment office thinks you'd be one over quota," he chuckled.

"Sorry, sir?" I asked, puzzled.

"If we hired you, he thinks we'd have one too many Irish Catholics."

Once more I could feel my dander rising, but Dunn raised a sooth-ing hand.

"Take it easy, young fellow."

He picked up his phone and dialed a number. When his call was answered, he said, "I have a man here by the name of McCormack. I understand he was down there talking to you earlier, is that so?"

There was a pause as the civilian supervisor responded.

"Well, he's a friend of mine. Did you know that?" Dunn snapped.

Again a pause.

"Now, I'm going to have a cruiser bring him right back down, and when he gets there I want you to treat him right. *Do you understand me?*"

Apparently he did because I was hired that very day. God bless you, Jim Dunn!

It will surprise no one when I say that policing in a big city is much different from "fighting crime" in Bermuda. Nevertheless, many of the lessons I had absorbed during my five-year stint on the island stood me in good stead in my new career.

My first ten years on Metro were spent performing uniformed and plainclothes duties out of various downtown divisions, where most of the action took place. Along the way, I worked with and for an array of characters who were regarded not only by their fellow officers, but also by the rounders on the street, as legends. Naturally, my approach to homicide investigation was shaped by these men.

One of them was Kevin Boyd, my first plainclothes partner in the old 5 Division, which used to stand at the corner of Davenport Road and Belmont Street, in the very heart of the city. It was Kevin who, in a sense, initiated me into detective work in the mid-1960s — something I had never thought I would become involved in, believing my entire police service would be spent in uniform. He, perhaps more than any other police officer I ever worked with, shaped my attitudes towards criminal investigative work and helped me develop whatever abilities and talents I might have had for it. Kevin and I became close friends, and I was deeply saddened in 1980 when he was tragically killed in a car accident.

Another wonderful character who comes to mind from those early days was a big, tough sergeant of detectives by the name of Des Brian. Des had little use for orthodoxy, which is *not* to say he scorned proper police procedures or the law, but rather that he favoured using them in creative and enterprising ways. And his methods usually paid off. I'm proud, as so many others have been, to say that I was one of Des Brian's boys.

While working in the detective office, I came into contact with

PROLOGUE

Detective Sergeant George Thompson, a member of Metro's elite Homicide Squad. George seemed to like the way I handled myself, and arranged to have me seconded to Homicide so I could help him with a couple of murder investigations. As a probationary detective, I knew I was being auditioned and was determined to make the most of it. I also knew that probationary detectives seldom got a kick at Homicide. Moreover, to be accepted into the squad, I needed what was irreverently referred to on the force as a "rabbi" – someone on the inside who would vouch for me. George Thompson had evidently appointed himself my rabbi, and I couldn't have had a better one. He was one of the city's top homicide investigators, a man whose reputation for painstaking thoroughness and airtight case preparation had earned him the respect of senior police officers and defence attorneys alike. George was a patient but demanding mentor who insisted that things be done in a fair and open manner.

I recall once objecting strenuously to his unorthodox suggestion that we provide the lawyer representing a man accused of a particularly gruesome murder with a copy of the crown brief. Police officers weren't in the habit of tipping their hand to the bad guy's mouthpiece. When I voiced my reluctance, George's response was blunt: "Let me put it this way, Bill: Give him the damned brief!" I did as I was ordered and soon learned that it was the best thing we could have done. The defence lawyer knew and trusted George. When he saw the evidence that the crown intended to call, he acknowledged that his client was a done goose. We got a conviction.

A longtime partner of mine from the Homicide Squad, Herm Lowe, was as decent and compassionate a human being as I'm ever likely to meet in this life. Herm had been on the RCMP, but left the horsemen after seven years to join Metro. Our paths crossed when he was transferred into Homicide in 1975 to act as my partner. By that time, I'd been promoted to detective sergeant and was one of the veterans of the squad. Together, we investigated scores of murders. With Herm Lowe, more than any other partner I worked with, I shared everything there was to experience on Homicide. And as I prepare to share some of our stories, I deeply regret he isn't still here to lean across the desk and tell me, in his straightforward, down-east way, how utterly full of bullshit I am. Herm died of cancer in 1988.

But another fondly remembered Homicide partner of mine, Jack McBride, still doesn't hesitate to take me down a peg or two with the raspy sense of humour that kept us both sane in the midst of grim situations. Seldom has there been a more meticulous investigator than Jack, who used to delight in reminding me – and just about everybody else in the squad – that he'd been a traffic man. In fact, a number of Homicide Squad members were former traffic accident investigators. They fit well into the squad because they were accustomed to major investigations involving scene preservation, evidence gathering, statement taking, postmortems, and all the other minutiae involved in preparing and presenting a major case in court.

All of these men were good police officers, seasoned investigators at the top of their game. They knew Toronto intimately and loved the city. Like me, none of them would have wanted to do police work anywhere else. Besides, life on Homicide is the same no matter where you go, as are the rationalizations with which killers everywhere justify the taking of a life. It doesn't matter if it's New York, Sydney, London, or Toronto, murder is just as ugly, death is just as final, and the ensuing human devastation is just as tragic and profound.

In the years I spent on Homicide, I would discover the truth of George Sellar's admonishment to me my first day on the squad. As he had warned, I would encounter horrors that were beyond my own imagination to conceive. And just as George had foreseen, Jean and I would struggle to keep our family life from being overwhelmed by the punishing hours and the unrelenting diet of misery that life on Homicide dished up.

In the pages that follow, I tell the stories behind a number of the homicides that my partners and I investigated. It's important to remember that every one of these real life dramas took place in "Toronto the Good," a fact which I'm sure will be unsettling to readers who call Toronto home. I've tried to convey what it was really like for us to deal with the most serious of crimes, day in and day out, usually under a media spotlight. I've attempted to explain how it felt to work virtually round the clock, sometimes for days on end, to solve a particularly difficult or brutal case, only to see the murderer receive a sentence so light that the victim's family was denied even the pretence of justice.

Readers will follow my partners and me into places they'd never willingly venture themselves – murder scenes and police stations, jail cells and bawdyhouses, the city morgue and hospitals for the criminally insane, courthouses and the back alleys and dives where pimps, thieves, drug dealers, break-in artists, and all manner of other bandits hang out. This is the world of the homicide investigator.

In revisiting these cases – a cross section of the dozens of homicides I encountered on the squad – I've done my best to be faithful to the truth, and to draw the clearest possible picture of what life is like on this elite investigative unit of the Metropolitan Toronto Police Force. Having said that, for reasons of privacy and compassion I have deliberately disguised the identities of some of the characters who appear in a few of the stories. I have not, however, altered in any way the actual circumstances surrounding the homicides themselves or the evidence that ultimately led to the arrests and convictions of the killers.

As a final word, I want to remind readers of George Sellar's injunction to me not to be seduced by the glamour associated with homicide work. It was good advice for it helped me to keep things in perspective, especially when reporters came looking for a story. A sense of perspective and an honest humility are desirable attributes in all of us, and police officers are no exception. I've always believed that these two qualities are embodied in the Metropolitan Toronto Police Homicide Squad motto, which I strove to live by for all those years: "We speak for the dead to protect the living."

WJM
TORONTO

1

Rule Number One

F *rom time to time, members of the Homicide Squad were called upon to investigate the death of a known criminal, or even a fellow police officer. These exceptions aside, we seldom knew the victims in cases we investigated. However, on one occasion in 1970, I did happen to be personally acquainted with the murder victim and may have come within a hair's breadth of becoming one myself.*

Trevor Poll was a kind-hearted man who thought the best of just about everybody. He bussed tables, swept floors, and washed dishes at Fran's, a well-known eatery that used to stand on the west side of Yonge Street, a short block north of Dundas. A skinny little gnome who bustled about the place in his white apron, chattering eagerly in quick staccato bursts about nothing in particular to anybody who'd listen, the forty-year-old Poll was well known to Fran's regulars. Like its sister restaurants of the same name dotted around Toronto, the downtown Fran's was a respectable establishment that welcomed shoppers and business people – and Metro police officers – in search of a reasonably priced meal served in clean, pleasant surroundings.

The main floor restaurant was a casual, somewhat hectic place, but on the second floor, which contained three connecting rooms, the decor and ambience were decidedly tonier. In Le Salon, businessmen in well-cut suits sipped highballs. A few feet away, in the Ox Red Grill, couples dined off bone china set on linen tablecloths, then wandered into the Francis Room to listen to a small jazz combo and take a slow turn around the dance floor before calling it a night. Downstairs at Fran's you ate; upstairs you dined and were entertained.

The street-level restaurant catered to a more varied clientele, including patrons of the Funland arcade next door, a tough and riotously noisy joint that reeked then, as it does now, of sweat and cigarette smoke. The arcade is nothing more than a long, narrow stall composed of three grungy walls, a bare ceiling from which fluorescent lights and cables hang, and a grimy glass entrance opening onto Yonge. The incessant roar of the pinball and video games that line all three walls make it virtually impossible for unwelcome ears to intercept the furtive negotiations of buyers and sellers of everything from stolen goods to street drugs. Over the years, a lot of under-the-table deals went down at Funland.

Trevor loved his job at Fran's, and he was fascinated by police. It didn't matter whether you were the newest uniformed rookie walking the beat or a seasoned veteran working plainclothes, he'd want to know all about your latest pinch. And if he happened to know the bandit you'd arrested, which was highly probable because word travels fast on the Yonge Street Strip, he'd shake his head vigorously in absolute disbelief that "such a nice guy, such a nice guy! Comes in here all the time, ya know. Oh my gosh! Hell of a nice guy" could have done whatever it was that had earned him a trip to the slammer.

He worked steady nights, staying behind to clean up the place after everyone else had gone home. He scrubbed pots and pans until dawn while he listened to the portable radio that was his only companion. I'd often see him walking back to his little room on Gerrard Street around eight or nine in the morning, where he lived by himself. Sometimes I'd stop to give him a lift, and on those occasions he'd always ask me in for a coffee, but I never took him up on it.

A funny, innocent little guy, who meant no harm to anyone.

But there were limits to Trevor's generosity of spirit. When hoods broke into the restaurant through the third-floor skylight one April night in 1970, they were surprised by the equally startled but enraged bus boy who somehow found the courage to challenge them. Soon, the biggest of them recovered his wits sufficiently to begin slugging Trevor across the face and head with a blackjack before throwing him to the floor and running out the back door. Trevor's brush with danger brought him some cuts and bruises, but it also earned him a measure of celebrity along the strip – something the little man clearly relished.

"Hey! D'ya see my name in the paper?" he liked to brag after the incident. "I heard them guys breakin' in and put the run on 'em. Damn right! I scared them bastards off, ya know. The big bugger slugged me across the head with somethin'. If I ever see him again, I'll drop him, sonofabitch!"

In fact, we learned later that his attackers took off because they hadn't realized that the 120-pounder, who in reality had screamed in terror while he was being beaten, was all alone. After the break-in, he decided to keep a flashlight handy while he worked – ineffectual protection in what was then the heart of Toronto's underworld.

Most of the coppers and rounders who worked the downtown

Yonge Street Strip knew each other and operated on a first-name, but by no means cordial, basis. Among the street people who hung out on those corners, a pecking order existed, a kind of hierarchy with bikers and other heavies at the top, and drug-addicted hookers and scared runaway kids from the suburbs or small towns at the bottom. Regardless of one's position on the ladder, survival in this part of the city depended on following two simple rules: number one, don't take on anybody stronger than you; number two, keep your mouth shut.

Office towers and upscale stores built in the 1980s and early 1990s have since replaced the soot-stained commercial buildings and run-down rooming houses that used to line the streets running off Yonge, completely changing the character of the area immediately adjacent to the Strip. Until the 1970s, this was a neighbourhood of sleazy hotels that rented rooms by the hour (no questions asked), flophouses that harboured hopeless men, and crummy little shops that sold used office furniture, sex appliances, army surplus, and cheesy designer knock-offs. Still, despite its down-at-heel daytime appearance, on a hot summer night the Strip throbbed with an intoxicating energy.

Sidewalks crammed with thousands of shuffling people: wisecracking teenaged boys intent on impressing their giggling girlfriends with harebrained stunts that sometimes landed them in the back seat of a police cruiser; middle-class suburbanites walking off dinner at George's or Barberian's; ragged down-and-outers panhandling for enough change to buy a couple of watered-down drafts at one of the half-dozen crummy taverns in the area; pub-crawling university students shambling boisterously between rough-and-tumble watering holes like the Zanzibar and the Brown Derby; smart-assed street kids, twelve or thirteen years old, hanging out the back windows of the Dundas streetcar as it rumbled through the intersection to gawk and whistle at the mini-skirted hookers working the "track," unofficially circumscribed by George, Shuter, Gerrard, and Yonge Streets.

Before the Eaton Centre was built – partially in an attempt to make the intersection commercially respectable – Yonge and Dundas had a carnal energy that acted as a magnet for every drug dealer, booster, petty thief, and hooker in the downtown area. The arcades, alleyways, and bars near this busiest of intersections were clearinghouses for the cash exchange of sex, drugs, stolen property, guns, phony identification – you name it. If it was illegal or "sinful," it was for sale at Yonge and Dundas.

Uniformed beat cops who hadn't yet lost their appetite for street action wouldn't trade the stretch of sidewalk from College to Queen for any other in the city. Of course, in the centre of it all was Funland. That's where I did a lot of business.

During the 1960s, I worked General Assignment in the detective office at 52 Division, at 149 College Street, a building that today houses some facilities of the Ontario College of Art. My partner at the time was Doug Monteath, as good a street copper as you'll ever find, and a sharp investigator. We were cruising by Funland one Friday night when I spotted three known rounders who were just about to go inside. Doug was driving, and I told him to pull over to the curb. As soon as the car stopped, we both got out and shook them down. I told one of them to stand with his back to a storefront, and not to move a muscle, while Doug and I talked to the other two: "Where've you been? When did you leave there? Go anywhere else? Where are you heading? I thought your probation order said you weren't supposed to hang out with these assholes." That sort of thing.

Not surprisingly, each of them gave us a different story, leading us to search them as they stood with their hands on top of the cruiser. One had a screwdriver, another a pair of pliers, the third a wad of cash and some change. We scooped them for possession of burglar tools and took them back to the station. Within an hour, one had guided us to a house in a fashionable neighbourhood in the city's north end. He admitted that he and his buddies had broken in and taken some cash and expensive jewelry, including a woman's Cartier wristwatch. We had the cash and some of the jewelry, but what had they done with the watch?

"You know when you were searching me beside the police car?"

"Yeah, what about it?"

"I stuffed it in the rain gutter on the top of the cruiser."

And that is exactly where we found it, still ticking!

We cleared up more than twenty housebreaks over the next couple of days, and all because we kept a watchful eye on people going in and out of Funland.

By the 1970s, I had moved on from plainclothes to the Homicide Squad, and used to have coffee at Fran's fairly often — mostly on afternoon shifts, or when I was trolling the Strip for one hood or another. I'd often bump into Trevor Poll and we'd gab for a few minutes as he scurried between the kitchen and the lunch counter, collecting dirty dishes and dumping coffee grounds.

One June night, about two months after he'd first been attacked, a gang of thieves broke into Fran's again. And as before, Trevor was all alone.

He was found in the morning with his skull crushed by numerous blows from a pry bar that had been left behind. Fragments of bone protruded from his bloodied and matted hair like broken crockery, and the savagery of the blows had knocked out his dentures. They were found on the floor several feet from his body. This time there would be no regaling customers with stories of defiance in the face of danger. Instead, there was only a dismal little funeral service paid for by the restaurant owner and attended by a handful of employees and coppers who barely knew him.

The case was assigned to me, and to George Thompson, with whom I'd already worked on a number of investigations. George was the epitome of the homicide investigator. He knew the Criminal Code thoroughly from back to front, and used to delight in starting arguments over it. To many officers outside the Homicide Squad – especially the hard-bitten uniformed staff sergeants who really run police stations (regardless of what their inspectors believe) – he could be infuriatingly demanding, even high-handed, when it came to arbitrarily diverting officers from their normal chores to run errands for us in the midst of our investigations. Just under six feet tall, not a hair out of place, and dressed impeccably in suits one would expect to find hanging in the closets of well-paid chief executives, George exuded a panache and savoir-faire most people found hard to resist.

He was at his theatrical best whenever he encountered resistance from certain kinds of people, especially self-proclaimed intellectuals, or those who threatened to invoke powerful business or political connections to get their way. At such times, he would swell to his full height and remind them in an ominous tone that he was "Staff Sergeant George Thompson of the Metropolitan Toronto Police Homicide Squad. I am involved in an investigation of the most serious kind: the murder of a human being. And I want to remind you also that I am the Coroner's Constable. If you do not wish to have these premises and everything and everyone inside it, including you, impounded, I suggest that you cooperate, *and right now!*" George was a marvelously accomplished bullshitter of the first water!

But not on the morning he and I stood surveying the scene in Le Salon, where the bus boy's bloodstained body lay with a tablecloth twisted around his neck, causing his grossly misshapen head to loll to one side.

"He looks small, doesn't he? Like a kid." George didn't continue. He looked solemnly down at Trevor for a moment or two, then resumed writing in his notebook without saying a word for several minutes. George had known Trevor Poll, too.

Trevor's murder appeared to be a break and enter gone bad. A preliminary list of suspects would likely include just about every known shopbreaker in this part of the city. Word went out to the beat officers and to the boys working "old clothes," the ones known as the alley rats because it is hard to distinguish them from the bad guys, that we had a whodunnit on our hands. Overnight, the rounders on the strip — especially those with previous arrests for B&E — couldn't turn around without a police officer backing them up against a wall and asking where they'd been, what they'd been up to, and where they were going. In the language of the street, coppers from all downtown Toronto divisions rode the rounders' asses raw. Criminals hate being rousted like that, but we were determined to get results.

Within a few days, we got a tip from the Intelligence Bureau that a five-man B&E team had been active in the area recently. George was all for rounding them up, assuring me, "They'll tell us what we want to know."

We hauled them in one at a time. The first guy had an alibi. So did numbers two and three. The fourth guy wouldn't give us the time of day, and by the time we got to number five, we knew we weren't going to get anywhere – at least not this way. So we tapped their phones and bugged one of their places, then sat back to listen.

We didn't have long to wait because as soon as the bandits walked through their door, they hollered into ceiling fixtures, hot air ducts, wall receptacles – anything that might conceal a microphone – "Hi, Bill! Hey, George! How's it goin'?" We then had to endure several minutes of catcalls and guffaws, and listen to mock confessions to everything from the theft of the Stanley Cup to the kidnapping of Elmer the Safety Elephant – both of which had actually happened in recent years.

We thought we'd come up empty this time, but we were wrong. The gang members knew the heat was on, and they didn't like being squeezed. They were especially edgy about being questioned by homicide detectives. Murder is a heavy beef, and they wanted no part of it. They decided to feed us some information so we'd back off and leave them alone. One of them came to our office. "I got a name for you," he offered.

The name, which I'm not at liberty to reveal, led us straight to Funland. The Break and Enter Squad did a lot of spade work there on our behalf. They had a good idea of who was active, who was inside doing time, and who was out on bail facing charges and under pressure to pull even more jobs to pay their lawyers. They also had a solid knowledge of the various methods of entry – what's known as the *modus operandi*, or MO – that each shopbreaker, or team of shopbreakers, used. Their MOs, which included the tools they used, were their signatures.

Because we knew that the man whose name we'd been given hadn't done the April Fran's job alone, we asked members of the B&E Squad to up the heat on the rounders at Funland, and to make their lives very uncomfortable, indeed. I remember asking one of the B&E boys how things were going over there. He flashed a wicked grin and said, "When they see us coming, they scramble for the door in search of any rathole they can find. We're about as popular in that place as a spare prick at a wedding!"

Our persistence soon paid off. Within a week of Trevor Poll's murder, George and I had arrested a Funland employee who admitted to having planned, with two other employees, the April break-in, during which Trevor had been injured. He told us who else was in on the job, and we issued warrants for their arrest. A little over a week later, the second suspect was arrested while driving on the Don Valley Parkway. But the third man – the one who'd blackjacked Trevor, the same one we'd gotten the tip about – was still on the loose.

He was a new employee at Funland, an American who hadn't yet come to the attention of Canadian police, though, as we would soon find out, it wasn't for lack of trying. We checked him out through the FBI in New York City and learned he was well known in Brooklyn for car theft, wife assault, armed robbery, and escaping custody. Previous addresses included Sing Sing Prison.

In the short time he'd been living in Toronto, he had successfully established a reputation among minor members of the underworld as a heavy you didn't mess with. He cultivated his mystique by dressing and talking differently from the rest of the riffraff. He forsook their denim and leather in favour of stylish sports clothing that accentuated his athletic physique. His accent was a languid blend of Caribbean patois and southern drawl. The two men we had in custody regarded him as the brains behind the operation, a predator whom they were loath to cross.

They told us the third man had badly injured his leg during the April break-in, and that after having the leg set the next day in the Wellesley Hospital Emergency Room, had torn the cast off before taking the train to Calgary and then on to Vancouver to lie low for several days. But when he returned to Toronto, he was short of cash and, in rapid succession, pulled a number of armed robberies. One of his associates – a crooked shop owner who would soon find himself behind bars as a co-conspirator – was certain the American would be fingered for the June break-in at Fran's and, thus, for Trevor Poll's murder. He urged his colleague to leave the city again as soon as he could.

So suspect number three headed for Hamilton, where he robbed a trust company at gunpoint, then took the train to Montreal. And that's where we caught up with him – or, to be more precise, where members of Montreal's Hold-Up Squad caught up with him.

We'd received a tip that he'd taken a room at the Towne Squire Motel, so we telephoned the Montreal police, who obliged us by paying the man a surprise visit – an event that he later told us had left an indelible impression on him. I think what impressed him most about the abrupt, to say nothing of rude, appearance by a number of heavily armed Montreal detectives in his shabby room was the instant and explosive transformation of a seemingly substantial motel room door into a chaotic heap of kindling. He later admitted to George and me, when he was safely back in Toronto, that after the Montreal police burst through his door it had taken him several seconds to catch his breath, and several more minutes before his teeth stopped chattering long enough for him to ask to use the washroom.

Once back in Toronto, the man and his associates were charged with numerous criminal offences, which included armed robbery, break and enter, fraud, and conspiracy. But they were not charged with the murder of Trevor Poll, for one simple reason: they hadn't done it.

Nor had a lot of other criminals who were caught in the wide net we cast in our search for Trevor Poll's murderers. But that didn't prevent us from charging them with a long list of offences that kept a couple of dozen members of the Criminal Bar busily and gainfully occupied for many months to come. That's often how it goes in such investigations. If you shake enough trees, eventually something will fall out and surprise you.

Our best piece of evidence in the Trevor Poll murder remained the brand-new pry bar that had been used to jimmy the second-floor back door of Fran's and to bludgeon Trevor to death. When discovered at the scene, it still bore the price tag of a local hardware store just a few blocks away. Putting that murder weapon in the hands of the person responsible for taking Trevor's life would involve many months of hard slogging, and would take us far beyond the Yonge Street Strip. Investigations such as this one are exercises in patience. They demand strict attention to detail, and testify to the tedium that comprises much of police work. They are woven from many unremarkable and seemingly unrelated strands, and the task is finished only when these strands hang together tightly enough to absolutely convince a jury.

The first tenuous strand in the Trevor Poll case was a supposedly innocuous speeding ticket issued three days before his murder. Constable David Moorley was sitting in his police cruiser on Woodbine Avenue, south of Queen Street, thinking that if he had to operate radar on a warm spring day, it might as well be here, where he could enjoy the cool breeze blowing off Ashbridge's Bay.

A little after noon, the radar machine began to whine, indicating that he had a customer. Moorley hopped out of the cruiser and flagged down a speeding brown Chev whose driver reluctantly pulled the car over to the curb. Moorley wrote out a ticket and handed it to the driver, one Nicholas Popovic, who told the officer he'd rented the car earlier that day from an agency at Yonge and Dundas. Popovic angrily snatched the ticket from Moorley's hand, then drove away. Nothing suspicious about that. After all, who likes to get dinged for speeding, especially on a nice spring day?

The second strand was less tenuous and certainly more interesting. Fourteen hours after Moorley nabbed his speeder, Constable Paul Bushe of 43 Division spotted a brown Chev with four men in it parked behind some shrubs in the area of Kingston and Markham Roads, a commercial area in the city's east end. He called for a back-up, and when the second officer arrived, he and Bushe approached the car to question the occupants.

The driver identified himself as twenty-nine-year-old Nicholas Popovic. He was a small, slender man with slow, lazy eyes and a malignant scowl. He didn't try to disguise his contempt for Bushe, and gave evasive answers to the constable's questions. In the car with Popovic were twenty-four-year-old Elija Askov, a slight man with the face and furtive demeanour of a rodent; a barrel-chested twenty-nine-year-old man who called himself Milos Cveticanin and sat impassively in the back seat of the car, speaking only when Bushe addressed him directly; and twenty-four-year-old Radko Govedarov, a slightly built six-footer who smoked nervously and never took his eyes off Bushe or his partner.

Each was asked to step out of the car one at a time, until all four men had been questioned separately about their presence in the area so late at night. The two policemen had worked the streets long enough to know when someone was trying to deceive them, and the story this quartet tried to feed them was pure bullshit. Neither Popovic nor his passengers realized, however, how intriguing bullshit can be to seasoned police officers, who find nothing so fascinating or worthy of their attention as a barefaced lie on the lips of a rounder at two in the morning.

When good coppers can't immediately figure out what their suspects are up to, they prudently back off and give the criminals more of the proverbial rope they need to hang themselves. And that's what Bushe and his partner did. They recorded their encounter with the four men on what are known as Persons Investigated Cards, let the men go, and submitted these cards at the end of their shift.

The break-in during which Trevor Poll was murdered would not occur until two days after Popovic and his confreres were checked out on Kingston Road. When the break-in and Trevor's body were discovered, the cards that Bushe and his partner submitted on Popovic and his associates became very important.

In those days, all police records were maintained and referenced manually – the computer age was still on the horizon. Persons Investigated Cards were routinely sent to the Records and Inquiry Bureau (RIB) at the end of each shift. There civilian records personnel with astonishing memory skills read and cross-filed them on huge revolving drums. Working on the Homicide Squad, I got into the habit of wandering into RIB for a coffee and a chat with Gary Rossiter, Norm Lee, or one of the others working there, about who'd been checked out in a certain locality at a certain time. Sometimes I needed to know where I might find somebody I was looking for, whom he hung out with, what kind of car he drove. And more times than I can remember, before I'd drained my coffee cup, they'd have rolled the big drums backward and forward and, from among tens of thousands of cards, plucked out the answer they already knew was there.

Computers can't do that, only people can. I owe much to the civilian members of the force that I've worked with over the years, and I'm convinced that police officers labouring today in the computer age sometimes do so under a distinct disadvantage.

A third strand in the Poll case also emerged, even more interesting than the second. At the scene of another B&E unrelated to Fran's, identification officers lifted a fingerprint belonging to Radko Govedarov, one of the occupants of Popovic's rented car. Also intriguing was the discovery at the scene of a brand-new pry bar, complete with the price tag. His "signature" had made Radko Govedarov our prime suspect.

We sent Doug Lewis and Harry Wright of the B&E Squad to Popovic's home on Euclid Avenue to ask him where Govedarov could be found. Popovic bluffed his way through Lewis and Wright's visit, telling them he'd never heard of Govedarov and denying being found in his company in the rented Chev. Even when the officers showed him police photos of Govedarov, Popovic vehemently denied knowing him, telling Lewis and Wright to get lost.

Pay dirt! We were getting warm and we knew it!

When Lewis knocked on Elija Askov's door on Manning Avenue, he got a somewhat warmer reception. Yes, Askov knew Govedarov, and yes, he remembered being found in his company in 43 Division by the two uniformed policemen. As to where Govedarov could be found, Askov suggested that Lewis nose around the clubs and other hangouts frequented by members of the Eastern European underworld near Queen and Parliament Streets.

All that hot summer and into the fall, we kept an eye open for Govedarov, hoping that either Popovic or Askov would lead us to him. We had to be content with the waiting game because we didn't have enough to arrest either of them. Besides, if we had taken Govedarov's only known associates out of commission, we would have had no way of landing him. We just had to be patient and hope he'd surface.

He did. In Los Angeles.

It was a muggy August evening when Sergeant Bill Schmidt of LAPD's Rampart precinct, cruising alone in his patrol car along the seedy downtown streets, got a call to a fight near the intersection of 9th Avenue and Westmoreland. As he rolled to a stop, he saw a man detach himself from a knot of people milling about the sidewalk and begin running away. Schmidt got out of his police car without waiting for a back-up and gave chase, thereby breaking the cardinal rule of policework in that city of seven million souls, many of whom are armed.

Suddenly, the man spun around and opened fire on Schmidt with a handgun, striking the officer in the arm and chest. Schmidt went down, but he was still able to return the fire and hit the man in the chest, arm, and leg. More police cars and ambulances arrived at the scene within minutes, but by that time the man who had shot Schmidt had managed to drag himself beneath a parked car, where he lay badly wounded but still armed.

For several minutes, it was a standoff. The suspect lay under the car cursing the police and threatening to shoot anybody who got too close. Eventually, he began to succumb to loss of blood. The police seized the opportunity to move in long enough to attach a cable to the car, which they then proceeded to winch to uncover his prone body. They descended on him with guns drawn, and doubtless would have put more lead into him if he'd so much as twitched an eyebrow. But by then, the fight was out of him, and he lay bleeding on the pavement, drifting in and out of consciousness.

The police scooped up the man who just moments before had tried to kill one of their own, and tossed him onto the stretcher of a waiting ambulance. He and Schmidt were taken to Los Angeles County

General Hospital, where they underwent emergency surgery. While doctors were confident the police officer would recover fully, they weren't giving the same odds to the other man. A search of his blood-soaked clothing turned up identification in the name of Radko George Govedarov, a twenty-eight-year-old Bulgarian national who had apparently entered the United States illegally from Canada.

Investigators from the Rampart precinct telephoned Toronto to tell us they had Govedarov in the jail ward of the hospital. They said that if and when he recovered from his wounds, they intended to prosecute him for the attempted murder of Sergeant Schmidt. George Thompson told them that we wanted a chance to question him, but appreciated the fact that we'd have to await his recovery. Four and a half months later, in mid-January, George was on a plane bound for Los Angeles.

The Los Angeles County General Hospital is a massive building. The jail ward takes up one entire wing of the thirteenth floor, with beds for sixty patients. Since the shooting incident with Sergeant Schmidt, Radko Govedarov had occupied one of them. During that time, he'd undergone a number of surgeries and an extended period of convalescence, which included lying for days on end in traction to repair a shin bone that had been shattered by one of Schmidt's slugs. By the time Govedarov was well enough for George to interview him, he had become impatient with his doctor's advice to stay in bed, and had begun hopping around the jail ward.

On one such occasion, Tom Summers, a U.S. Army nurse assigned to the jail ward, had tried to encourage Govedarov to get back into bed because he was likely doing harm to his leg. The man seemed extremely depressed, and in response told Summers that it didn't matter what damage he might be doing because he was probably going to spend the next twenty or thirty years in jail anyway. Summers noted

Govedarov's emotional state and the substance of their conversation on his medical chart.

George met Govedarov and interrogated him over the course of three days. On the third day, he showed the fugitive a statement given by another member of the Eastern European underworld who had taken up residence in Toronto. The man claimed Govedarov had admitted to him that he had planned and carried out the break-in at Fran's with Popovic, Askov, and a third unknown man whom Govedarov called "Lucky," and that he, Govedarov, had beaten the bus boy to death with the pry bar. When confronted with this, Govedarov realized the jig was up and dictated a lengthy confession to George that ran to over thirty pages.

We had Govedarov, for whom extradition proceedings would soon begin, but what of the other three – especially the man he called Lucky?

Popovic and Lucky had gone to ground somewhere, so we assigned two solid street coppers from the Emergency Task Force, John Booth and Ken Greer, to stake out Elija Askov's place on Manning Avenue. For several months, they secretly watched his comings and goings in the hope that Popovic, Lucky, or both, would appear.

One of the places Booth and Greer followed Askov to, in the course of their surveillance, was a pool hall on College Street. They waited until Askov left, then interviewed the owner in an effort to ascertain the identity of Lucky. The owner agreed to accompany them to Police Headquarters where Lucky was positively identified, by means of photographs, as Streto Dzambas – the surly barrel-chested man who, months before, had told Police Constable Bushe his name was Milos Cveticanin. Arrest warrants were issued for Popovic and Dzambas, but not for Askov. Leaving him on the loose had led us to Dzambas's true identity. Who knew what else might come of leaving him on the street? Booth and Greer kept watch.

We wouldn't know until months had passed that Popovic and Dzambas were sweltering in the merciless heat of a south Texas jail near the Mexican border, awaiting trial on a charge of break and enter. They, like Govedarov, had fled Canada after the Fran's break-in – he to Los Angeles, they to Houston, where, in the wee hours of a January morning, they were caught by police inside a grocery store they had broken into.

Popovic told Houston police detectives that his name was Mike Novak, and Dzambas identified himself as Jany Odak. Back at the station, the team of "Novak" and "Odak" admitted to investigators that they had entered the United States illegally from Canada. They appeared in court the next day, where a judge ordered them held in custody. The jail in which the two men cooled their heels housed three hundred illegal aliens awaiting deportation from the United States. In the course of their investigation, Texas authorities were able to discover the men's true identities by matching fingerprints both American and Canadian police had on file. That's when we got a call.

By then it was July 1971, thirteen months after Trevor Poll had been killed. George boarded another plane, this time for Brownsville, Texas, where he met with officials who held Popovic and Dzambas in custody. Extradition proceedings for both men had begun the previous month. They were returned to Toronto in mid-July, where they gave me a full confession of their involvement in the incident that led to Trevor Poll's death. The only man still at large was Elija Askov. Booth and Greer scooped him without incident as he walked across the road near his Manning Avenue house.

It was Streto Dzambas who guided George and me through the break-in at Fran's. While George drove the police cruiser, Dzambas directed us up Yonge Street, where he pointed out the restaurant. He then pointed to the spot where he and the others had parked the rented Chev that PC Bushe had found them in two nights before the break-in. Together, we traced the gang's steps along connecting alleyways that led to the rear entrance of Funland, where he explained how they had mounted the roof at the back of Fran's and how they'd broken in. Inside the restaurant, Dzambas explained what had happened once they gained entry.

He told us that they had been surprised by the bus boy's presence so late at night, but that Govedarov had insisted on going ahead as planned because he was prepared to "take care of anybody who got in their way." And take care of him he had. He struck Trevor over the head with the pry bar, but instead of falling down unconscious, Poll began to scream. He kept screaming as more blows rained down on his face and head.

Dzambas claimed that when he pleaded with Govedarov to stop hitting Poll, Govedarov responded by grabbing Dzambas and pulling him over Poll's now prone and bloodied body. For a brief moment, Dzambas thought Govedarov might strike him, too, but he didn't. Dzambas told us that when Poll wouldn't stop screaming, an enraged Govedarov grabbed a linen tablecloth, twisted it around Poll's neck, and used it as a tether to hold the bus boy fast while he beat him into a state of unconsciousness.

With Trevor's screams finally silenced, Govedarov reached into his victim's pants pocket and removed his wallet. Then he half-pushed, half-dragged Dzambas to the rear door, and together with the others they fled up the lane to the waiting car. Poll's wallet was found a day later, where Govedarov had tossed it after first removing two dollars.

At their trial, all four men were convicted of non-capital murder and sentenced to prison for life. That should have been the end of it, but it wasn't.

In late November 1974, Radko Govedarov of Joyceville Penitentiary decided to give himself an early Christmas present – an unauthorized release from custody. He did this by tunnelling to freedom under a perimeter fence. Authorities issued a warrant for his arrest, with a cautionary note that he was to be considered extremely dangerous.

On a blustery, cold Friday afternoon in January 1975, about seven weeks after the prison break, I got an anonymous tip that Govedarov had been seen in Toronto outside the Brunswick House, a well-known watering hole on Bloor Street near Bathurst. Instead of taking a police cruiser, my new partner, Jack McBride, and I decided to grab the westbound subway. When the train arrived at Bathurst Station, Jack and I got off and ascended the escalator. Who should be standing at the top of the escalator but Radko George Govedarov!

He spotted me and immediately bolted for the exit. Charging through the station doors, bowling over two elderly women, he ran onto Bathurst Street. He was nearly struck by a trolley bus that was entering the station, but he dodged it and headed straight for the lane that runs parallel to Bloor behind the shops and upstairs apartments on the street's north side. I forced my way through a double line of people who were filing into the station from the street. When I finally emerged onto the sidewalk, I saw him disappear down the alley. Jack was right behind me, so I shouted over my shoulder at him to get help, then gave chase.

Away from the simulated daylight of the busy nighttime street, with its neon signs and glaring car lights, the alley was a gloomy place. It took a few seconds for my eyes to adjust to the darkness. To make matters worse, the dirty snow that had accumulated in the alley bore the tracks of countless vehicles, and these had frozen into icy ruts that made footing treacherous. Once, my feet went right out from under me, and I skidded painfully on my side, scraping the skin off one of my shins.

I picked myself up in time to see Govedarov run across Markham Street and into the alley leading to Palmerston Avenue. He was about a hundred feet ahead of me. When he was halfway along this section of the alley, which was the darkest point, he suddenly stopped and ran back towards me. From my point of view, he was nothing more than a black silhouette against the dim light of Palmerston, another hundred feet beyond him. For one sickening moment, all I could think of was the Los Angeles Police Sergeant who had met Govedarov under exactly these circumstances.

But before he'd taken more than a few paces in my direction, Govedarov grabbed hold of the low-hanging ladder of an iron fire escape. With amazing agility, he swung his legs up and through the lowest rung of the ladder then, hand-over-hand, pulled the rest of his body up until he gained his feet and stood motionless on the bottom rung glaring down at me. I had continued running and was almost abreast of the fire escape when he looked frantically up to the rooftops, then down at me again, momentarily unsure of what to do next. By then, I was directly beneath him, and no more than ten feet away.

I yelled, "Give it up, Radko. Come on down!" I don't know how I got the words out because my mouth was as dry as a chip.

For a moment, both of us stood motionless, each trying to catch his breath, each wondering what the other was about to do.

Here was a dangerous criminal who had committed one murder, had attempted another, had escaped from prison, and was clearly a threat to the public. I had all the grounds I needed to draw my revolver, and that's exactly what I did.

With my gun pointed straight at his chest, I ordered him, once again, to come down. For what seemed like several minutes, but was probably just a few seconds, he looked at me as though he might surrender. Then he craned his neck to look up and down the dark, deserted alley.

If I holstered my gun and tried, as he had, to pull myself up onto the fire escape, I knew he'd have me at his mercy – and he certainly hadn't shown much of that in his criminal career. If I shot him (and from where I stood I couldn't miss) it would have been tantamount to a summary execution, given that I had no clear evidence that he was armed. I quickly decided that shooting him wasn't an option. I would just have to bluff.

"I told you to come down here. Now!"

"Fuck you!" he yelled, then turned and scrambled up the ladder before disappearing over the edge of a roof.

As I stood panting in the alley, I could hear him scrabbling noisily across the uneven roofs, banging into unseen objects, falling up wooden staircases, tripping over wires, and cursing. Trying to negotiate this treacherous terrain in the dark was no easy feat. I began to think that I didn't need to shoot my quarry: the miserable bastard would likely break his neck up there!

Within a few minutes, thanks to Jack's call, police cruisers, and plenty of them, converged on the area. The eyes of hundreds of passersby and of dozens of police officers, who by now had sealed off the short block between Markham Street and Palmerston Avenue, were fixed on the rooftops three stories aboveground. Everyone waited for something to happen.

In a third-floor apartment on the northwest corner of Markham and Bloor, a family of eight had just sat down to enjoy their Friday night supper. They were oblivious to the commotion taking place below. In the steaming tureen, which sat in the centre of their table, was the same delicious meal they enjoyed every Friday, everybody's favourite: a fragrant Caribbean stew called souse. No sooner had they offered up their thanks for the safe conclusion of their week, and for the meal they were about to share, when across the room the picture window that looked out onto the street exploded into countless vicious shards. Sprawled in the middle of their living room rug was a wild-eyed man who, having just launched himself through the window, was now in the process of picking himself up to flee.

The sudden shock of having their weekly meal interrupted in such breathtaking fashion galvanized every member of that family of eight. It was pandemonium! They fell upon the man with fist and foot and ladle. Even the youngest, an eight-year-old girl, landed a few furious licks to his head with a small camera suspended on a string. Seldom has such a thorough body and fender job been done on anyone! By the time a couple of uniformed boys from 14 Division got to him, a bruised and battered Radko Govedarov was only too happy to be arrested.

"These people crazy!" he moaned.

Later, as he was being led from the Homicide office, he turned to me and said, "McCormack, you lucky I don't shoot you, tonight."

Was this false bravado? Did he actually have a gun in that alley? I'll never know because we never found one.

"Well, Radko, I was going to say the same thing to you," I said as he limped out of the room between the two prisoner escort officers who'd been assigned to take him back to jail.

2

"Mister Johnnie Bolden"

Every murder represents a human tragedy. Not even the most hard-bitten police officer would disagree with that. But every now and then, homicide investigators are compelled to handle a case that descends far below the depths of tragedy to the realm of the profoundly grotesque, where the sights and the sounds and the smells are so horrific that they shock and sicken the most seasoned veteran. In May 1975, Herm Lowe and I investigated just such a case, the gruesome facts of which are not for the weak of stomach.

Standing six-foot-four and weighing over two hundred and fifty pounds, he was a mountainous human being. The unseasonably warm afternoon sun, which made it seem more like August than the middle of May, beat hot on his broad back, plastering his shirt to his body. The cardboard box he carried across Church Street was big enough to have contained a television set.

"He carried it like it was nothin'!" the woman recalled as she took a drag on her cigarette. She held her bony arms tightly across her chest and rocked back and forth in the chair. Still, she could not control the trembling. She saw me watching her and glared back resentfully. She had no love for the police, who had on numerous occasions tossed her husband into the bullpen to sober up. It had been almost a whole day since she herself had taken a drink, and irritability was giving way to panic.

Herm Lowe stood up and walked to the interview room door. "How would you like another cup of coffee?"

"Is that the best you can do?"

"Afraid so."

"Okay, but lotsa sugar this time. Don't forget."

"Lotsa sugar. Back in a minute."

Herm left the room, and I kept writing notes. Over the past few days, this pathetic, bedraggled woman sitting in front of me in the Homicide office, dressed in a faded floral smock and knee-high stockings with runs up both shins, had averted her eyes from sights that were so unimaginably horrible she had pretended to herself that they weren't real. But they *were* real, and as long as she lived, she would never be able to shake the memory of being forced to scrub the blood from the walls and floors of the big man's gloomy one-bedroom apartment, where he claimed there had only been a fight, a noisy argument with a woman.

But she knew this hadn't been just another drunken argument; there had been far too much blood for that.

In a moment, Herm returned with the coffee. He looked doubtfully at her, then at me, and shook his head. I knew exactly what he was thinking: How the hell are we ever going to keep her sober long enough to testify? And if she ever did take the box, even an inept defence lawyer would rip her to shreds.

I continued my questions. "Wasn't he afraid somebody might see him carrying that thing across the street?"

"It was Sunday," she said. "There weren't many people walkin' around, and there weren't many cars, either. Nobody'd think anything of it . . . except maybe me."

She went on to describe how he skirted the building on the corner of Monteith and Church and ducked into the small courtyard to the rear, which was enclosed on its east and west sides by three-storey-high brick walls, and on its north side by a six-foot wooden fence. Still clutching the box to his chest, he knelt down in the corner nearest one of the buildings. Then he cleared away some newspapers and pop cans that had accumulated there, folded back the flaps of the box and, reaching inside with both hands, pulled out a bulky, oddly shaped object about two and a half feet long swathed in a multicoloured bed-sheet. He propped his bundle against the fence.

"He stood up and flattened the box. Then he just kinda strolled casually, like nothin' was up, across Monteith Street to the back of the grocery store, and tossed the box into the dumpster. He never knew I seen him, but I did. I sure did! And I seen a lot more that morning." She shuddered and wiped a tear from a wrinkled cheek with the heel of a purple hand. "But I sure as shit wish I hadn't!"

The woman doubled over and began to dry retch between sobs. I reached over and touched her shoulder. She pulled away, needing comfort but not from me. Through chattering teeth, she said, "Either one of you guys got a smoke?"

Herm slid his opened pack along the desk. She took one and lit it with the cheap pink lighter she'd clutched in her hand since entering the interview room.

She was the last of many witnesses we had interviewed in this case, and it would take us another hour to extract from her all that she knew.

His name, whenever anybody asked him, was *Mister* Johnnie Bolden, but to the ragged down-and-outers who lived just a half step up from homeless in mouldering rooming houses near Church and Wellesley Streets, he was "The Dude." It was a handle he liked, fancying himself a lady-killer.

Johnnie Bolden was born in 1916 into a poor black sharecropping family who scrabbled in the dust of a sorrowful little speck on the map called Snow Lake, Arkansas. On his tenth birthday, his father decided he was big and strong enough to shoulder his share of the farm work, and pulled the boy out of school. In his teens Bolden fled the place he referred to with bitter contempt as "Niggertown, U.S.A.," and took up the life of a roustabout, thumbing rides from the cotton fields of Arkansas to the meat-packing plants of Chicago, and from the peach orchards of Georgia to the docks of New York City.

He possessed the strength of three men and was proud of it. There were periods over the years when he had used his generous endowment of muscle to earn an honest living. But there had also been many times when he had turned his might to the task of pounding the daylights out of somebody. Often his victims were women, and the savage beatings he administered usually landed them in hospital and him in jail. After one near fatal assault, during which he repeatedly raped, kicked, and punched a woman, he was sent to Sing Sing Prison for the better part of ten years. And just as he had every other time he was convicted, Bolden protested his innocence, insisting the victim, the police, and the prosecution witnesses were all out to get him.

"Mister Johnnie Bolden innocent! Wouldn't even hurt no fly!"

While he was in the joint, he was examined by a psychiatrist who concluded that he was suffering from a persecution complex and admitted him to the New York State Hospital for the Insane, at Dannemora. There, under the bemused eyes of his ward attendants, he spent hours tearing photographs of nude women out of *Playboy* magazines, which he would then ritually mutilate, creasing the image of each woman at both hip joints and then carefully tearing the photograph along the folds, thereby severing the woman's legs from her torso. Once the legs were removed, he folded them at the knees and tore them again so that each leg was in two pieces. As he bent over the photographs, he would croon softly and tunelessly to himself like a child totally absorbed in play.

In 1968, Bolden was released from custody and went to live in New York City. For three years, he worked on the docks as a stevedore. He left New York for Arkansas just one step ahead of the police, who wanted to question him about the disappearance of a woman. After an unhappy one-year stay in Little Rock, he headed north, and in June of 1972 he boarded a Greyhound bus and entered Canada near Montreal.

Bolden took another bus to Toronto. Within a few days of his arrival, he found his way to the Immigration office and applied for permanent resident status. While he awaited the results of his application, he rented a ground-floor apartment in Gloucester Mansions, a three-storey brown brick building on the southwest corner of Church and Gloucester Streets.

Bolden freely disclosed his appalling criminal record, which listed convictions and lengthy jail terms for no fewer than nine vicious assaults with fists, feet, knives, and steel pipes. Nevertheless, Canadian immigration officials somehow saw fit to allow him to remain in Canada. They even gave him a work permit. For the next few years, he kept mostly to himself and stayed out of trouble.

It was now mid-May 1975. Since arriving in Canada, Bolden had seldom been unemployed. And though he only knew how to do bull work, he was well paid for it. As a result, he always had a wad of money in his pocket – a fact that made him popular with the gaggle of booze-addled acquaintances who regularly jostled one another for a seat at his table in neighbourhood pisscans. Calling him "The Dude," they accepted his rounds of beer and listened to lewd and grisly tales of what he liked to do to women. But even this craven pack of wife beaters found it hard to stomach some of Bolden's graphic imagery.

Almost every weekday afternoon they would loiter on street corners until they saw him lumbering up Church Street on his way home from work. After the usual, "Hey, Dude, how's it goin'?" it would be into the nearest pub or, better yet, over to the beer store at Seaton and Gerrard where he might be cajoled into buying a couple of cases of Old Vienna. These he would hoist onto one of his massive shoulders as he strode past the covetous stares of derelicts sprawled on the benches and under the trees of Allan Gardens – hopeless men whose insides had been rotted by aftershave and melted shoe polish.

Among Bolden's grateful acquaintances was Noah Smoke, a fifty-three-year-old Micmac Indian who lived with his common law wife, Margaret Fraser, one block west of The Dude's apartment, on Gloucester Street. Over the past year, Smoke had many times sat with others and drunk himself into oblivion while The Dude held court. In recent months, though, he had begun to shy away – first, because he and his wife had started to attend Alcoholics Anonymous meetings, and second, because The Dude had made a number of salacious overtures to Margaret. Smoke was enraged, but he knew that if he dared to say anything, Bolden would beat him to a bloody pulp. He advised Margaret to keep away from the man.

Saturday, May 10 was warm and sunny. At about 3:30 p.m., a young couple was walking north up Church Street towards their Park Road apartment, after spending the day wandering around Centre Island. As they came abreast of the brown brick apartment building on the southwest corner of Gloucester and Church, a huge black man strode across their path. He was dressed in a manner that, in this neighbourhood at least, passed for style: beige bell-bottomed slacks, a white open-necked shirt, and a western-cut brown sports jacket. He was staring at a woman leaning languidly against the north wall of the building. She was white, in her late forties, tall, and perilously thin. She had sunken cheeks and the mottled complexion of one who has lived too long inside the bottle.

The man swaggered up to the woman and, reaching out, cupped her chin in both his hands and twice kissed her roughly on the lips. While she was being kissed, the woman mumbled incoherently. She did not return the man's affection, but she did not try to get away, either. Instead, she stood still, her back against the wall, staring up into the huge round face leering down at her. The scene unsettled the young couple. But this wasn't their problem, so they walked on.

Several minutes later, Garnet Smoke passed by the apartment building with his wife and children in the car. They were on their way to visit his brother Noah and his wife, Margaret. As they turned the corner at Gloucester, Garnet saw a tall black man kissing a woman whose bony shoulders he had pinned to the wall with his broad hands. Garnet drew his wife's attention to the couple, but neither said a word for fear their children, who had not observed the scene, would realize the woman being mauled was Margaret Fraser.

By the time Garnet and his wife reached Noah's front door, they had come to a hastily whispered agreement to say nothing about what they had seen. Both of them realized only too well that Noah seldom needed much of an excuse to slap Margaret around. There was no telling what he'd do to her when he found out she had been flirting with another man. After the usual greetings, Garnet tentatively asked Noah where Margaret was.

"Well, she went over to the Loblaw's on Church Street for a jug of milk, but *shit*, that was a while ago. I guess she'll be back soon."

It had always been painfully difficult for Garnet and his young family to spend much time in Noah and Margaret's filthy little bed-sitting room. Visits there were a matter of duty, not pleasure. Garnet used them to satisfy himself that his hard-drinking older brother had enough food in the fridge and sufficient money to pay the rent, and to encourage him to make even a half-hearted effort to take better care of himself. Garnet was worried about Noah's quickly deteriorating health, particularly the cancerous ulcers that had erupted like tiny volcanoes on his face and neck, and which bled freely because Noah was unable to stop picking at them.

Garnet didn't want to be around when Margaret came through the door. To avoid what would surely be an ugly scene, he and his wife took their children and left.

For the next few hours, Noah waited alone for Margaret to return. When she didn't materialize by nine o'clock, he called the police. But the radio room refused to send an officer to take the report. Noah and Margaret ran with a crowd that was well known for its marathon drinking bouts, during which one or another of the group would disappear for several hours, or even a few days, and end up sleeping it off in either a drunk tank or an alley. The officer on the other end of the phone assured Noah that Margaret would come back when she sobered up.

Noah had no choice but to wait for her. When she didn't show by one o'clock in the morning, he gave up and went to bed.

It was between two and three o'clock Sunday morning that David, the young man who lived in the apartment across the hall from Johnnie Bolden, returned home from his job at a downtown hotel. He was a fastidious and reticent man who mixed with no one in the building. Though only a narrow hallway separated their front doors, the two men lived lives that were worlds apart.

That morning, David made himself his habitual pot of herbal tea. It soothed him and helped him to sleep. On this particular occasion, however, his quiet ritual was disturbed by noises coming from Bolden's apartment. David could hear the deep, rhythmic drone of the man's voice. There was another noise, too. What was it? Gradually, it occurred to him that it was the sound of sawing. That was it, his neighbour seemed to be sawing small pieces of wood. But that made no sense. Why would he do that at this time of night?

David finished his tea and turned out the light. Within a few minutes, he was asleep.

Across the dark hall, the light burned in Johnnie Bolden's bathroom. Kneeling over a bathtub awash with blood, he crooned softly to himself as he methodically severed the legs from Margaret Fraser's horribly battered and disemboweled corpse. Every so often he jammed a carrot-sized finger into the drain to allow the dark gouts of blood that kept clotting there to escape.

One block west, Noah Smoke couldn't sleep. He was worried sick because Margaret still had not come home. At six o'clock he got out of bed, made a pot of coffee, and tried to figure out what to do next. After spending several fitful minutes occupying himself with pointless chores around the tiny apartment, he decided to go to mass at St. Basil's Church on Bay Street, a five-minute walk away. By half past seven, he was back home. Still no Margaret. He took their small dog out for a walk and didn't get back home again until half past eight. He scanned the Sunday paper, tuned in the news on the radio, even tried to distract himself by listening to records. None of it worked. He could feel the panic rising within him. He left the apartment and walked to the Devon Restaurant on Church Street for a cup of coffee.

Noah sat in the Devon for about an hour nervously smoking and trying in vain to think clearly. His nerves were shot, and the running sores on his face were itching fiercely this morning. He hadn't been able to keep his fingernails away from them. By the time he stood up to go, the front of his shirt was dotted with blood, but he couldn't have cared less. Though he desperately wanted a drink, he was just as desperately determined not to take one. His mind was on Margaret.

Noah decided to walk up and down every street in the neighbourhood until he found her. As he neared the corner of Church and Gloucester, The Dude stepped from the front door of his apartment building and called to him, inviting him to come in. Figuring Bolden might know something, Noah accepted the invitation and entered the apartment. As he crossed the threshold, he was struck by a pungent odour that he couldn't quite place.

Bolden took Smoke into the front room of the apartment, which was littered with empty beer bottles, and motioned for him to take a seat. He then disappeared into the kitchen, returning a moment later with two full bottles of beer. He handed one to Smoke, who placed it untouched on a steamer trunk that stood beside his chair.

Just as he started to explain that he was looking for Margaret, a woman wearing a faded floral smock entered the apartment without knocking and began to straighten out the rumpled sheets and blankets on a bed-chesterfield that lay open in the room. She was in her mid-fifties and very unsteady on her feet. Like Margaret, she had the wasted countenance and hangdog bearing of the compulsive drinker. She uttered not a word but kept to her work, occasionally casting fearful glances over her shoulder at the big black man whose stare never left her.

After she had smoothed the bedclothes, the woman struggled to fold up the bed-chesterfield, but it proved too much for her. She turned apprehensively to Bolden, who offered her no assistance, so Smoke stood up to help. It was then that he saw a pair of white running shoes that looked very much like the ones Margaret wore. They were on the floor near the wall. Noah felt the woman's eyes on him. But when he sought them out, he found them pleading in terror. Immediately, he understood that he must not let on to The Dude that he had seen the shoes. He nudged them with his foot until they were out of sight behind the bed-chesterfield.

Noah thought that if Margaret were anywhere to be found, this sonofabitch knew where to look. He decided to bide his time and, for the moment, say nothing to anyone. It was the safest thing to do.

As he and the woman were tucking away the bed-chesterfield, an unkempt middle-aged man Smoke took to be her husband entered the apartment. He too was drunk and, after grunting a general greeting to everyone, remained silent. Like his wife, he was deferential to Bolden, who handed the man and woman twenty dollars each before walking once more into the kitchen. As Bolden turned his back to leave the room, the man shot his hand out and snatched the woman's twenty, which he immediately pocketed with his own. She cast a poisonous glance at him.

Bolden heard and understood what had transpired behind his back.

"You sure a prick, Jackie, treatin' your woman that way. She worked for that money, scrubbin' an' cleanin'." Then he let loose a chesty laugh.

When he came back into the front room, he held an unopened case of beer aloft and, smiling beneficently at everyone, waved at them to follow him out of the apartment. The foursome walked kitty-corner across Church Street to the couple's tenement house a few doors up from Gloucester, where Smoke hoped he might at last find Margaret.

By the time they entered the couple's place, Bolden's ominous mood had completely given way to one of forced congeniality. Now, he was everybody's big brother; the kindly, generous Dude, the life of the party. He and the couple began tilting back the beer and listening to music. But Margaret wasn't around and nobody seemed to want to talk about her, so Smoke left.

Back at home, he lay down on his bed and tried to think. Why were Margaret's shoes at The Dude's place? Why hadn't he had the guts to confront him? What was he going to do now? Soon, he fell into a troubled sleep.

By four o'clock that afternoon, Smoke was awake. From somewhere he found the resolve to go back to Bolden's apartment to confront him. When the big man answered the door, it was clear that he was well and truly drunk and once again in a dangerously foul mood. Though he had said nothing about it when Smoke had visited him earlier in the day, Bolden raved on about how two women – one of them Margaret – had come to his apartment the night before, pried open the steamer trunk, and stolen two hundred and fifty dollars.

"There sho' nuff was a lot of screamin' goin' on in here, lass night!"

"Where's Margaret, Dude? Tell me where Margaret is."

"Margaret? Shit, man, how's I supposed to know? Ain't she *your* wife?"

Smoke left the apartment and walked to the nearby home of a friend, where he called the Don Jail to inquire whether Margaret had been brought in. He was told there was no prisoner there by that name. Then he called the police and asked to speak to the desk sergeant at the old 13 Division station near Bloor and Bathurst. Known among Toronto coppers as the Valley of the Dolls, it handled only women offenders. The switchboard operator put him through to the sergeant, who knew Margaret. But she wasn't there either. Smoke walked home, where he stayed for the rest of the night.

At about the time Noah Smoke had been on the line to 13 Division, Johnnie Bolden was seen by a wasted and terrified woman carrying a large cardboard box across Church and behind a building on the corner of Monteith Street.

At about two o'clock Monday morning, another curious incident was witnessed by a third-floor tenant of Johnnie Bolden's building. The man, who always slept with his bedroom window open, was awakened by a noise that came from the street below. When he went out onto his balcony to investigate, he saw Bolden pulling a light wire bundle buggy – the two-wheeled kind often used for grocery shopping – along the Gloucester Street sidewalk beneath his window. The wheels of the buggy squeaked loudly. Inside the buggy was a large green garbage bag that contained something hefty that the man could not make out. When Bolden got to the corner of Church and Gloucester, he crossed the deserted intersection diagonally until he came to the sidewalk on the far side. Then, still trailing the buggy, he walked north, coming to a stop in front of a row of tenement houses a few doors north of the intersection – the very building that Bolden, Smoke, and the drunken couple had entered Sunday morning.

There were common stairways at the front of these houses that gave access to both upper and lower levels, and at this hour they were shrouded in darkness. The man watched as Bolden snooped around one or two of the stairways. For one brief moment, he lost sight of him altogether. Bolden, after nosing around for several seconds, walked back across the street towards his own apartment building, pulling the now empty buggy behind him.

At six o'clock Monday morning, Noah Smoke got out of bed. Margaret had been gone now for more than a day and a half. He remembered that she was supposed to pick up a new lower plate at the denturists at Broadview and Gerrard that morning. He reckoned that she'd been out all weekend on a binge and was afraid to come home to him – at least that's what he hoped. She had probably sobered up enough by now and would likely keep her appointment with the denturist, he told himself. He decided to be on the doorstep as soon as the place opened.

At quarter to nine, Jeff, who operated a business on the corner of Monteith and Church Streets, poured himself a second cup of coffee and wandered out onto the fire escape of his third-floor office to relax and briefly enjoy the brilliant sunlit morning before getting down to work. In the warm months when the weather was fair, he often started his day this way, gazing out at the mature maple trees that lined many of the streets of this century-old neighbourhood. Lazily, his eyes traced the line of Monteith Street until they came to the blanket-sized yard that separated his building from the row of tenement houses immediately east of it. His attention was drawn to a suspicious-looking bundle lying on the ground almost directly beneath the fire escape on which he stood. It was a multicoloured bedsheet that enshrouded an oddly shaped object. The bedsheet was drenched in blood.

Jeff reluctantly walked downstairs and out the back door of his building to get a closer look. As he approached the bloody object, he was horrified at what he could see through a small gap in the bedsheet: a human hand curled up and over a blackened eye, as if to shade it from the glare of the morning sun. Seized with the urge to vomit, he ran inside to call the police.

About an hour after Jeff made what the papers would later refer to as a "gruesome discovery," Noah Smoke arrived at the denturist's office, intending to wait until Margaret turned up. He took a seat in the reception room beside two women who were talking about a radio news flash both of them had heard moments before – something about a woman's body being found behind a building on Church Street.

Noah didn't need to hear any more. In his heart, he knew they were talking about Margaret. He was overcome by despair and buried his face in his hands. When the receptionist asked if he was all right, he stood up and, without a word, left the building. Both she and the two women in the waiting room thought his behaviour was odd.

"And something else," said one later to the uniformed officer who'd been sent there to gather information about Noah. "There was fresh blood on his shirt."

"Yeah, fresh blood," said the other.

Within half an hour of the discovery of the body, Herm Lowe and I arrived at the scene. Bob Cook and Stan Neate of the 52 Division detective office were already there, and had done an excellent job of protecting things and deploying the two dozen uniformed officers who had been dispatched for crowd and traffic control. By the time we got there, they had already sealed off the streets in a two-block radius. Identification officer George Barrett was also on hand and had already photographed the body and the scene just as it was found by Jeff.

"Has the coroner arrived yet?" I asked George.

"Just got here. He's around back."

As soon as Dr. John Lovering formally pronounced death, I moved in closer.

"George, I'd like you to get shots of this."

Barrett continued photographing the body while I removed the bed-sheet and several sodden layers of newspapers that wrapped it. All the while, Herm stood off to one side taking careful notes and receiving exhibits as I handed them to him.

Herm: "One bedsheet with white and pink stripes, bloodstained; one piece of newspaper, *Toronto Star*, dated May 9, 1975, bloodstained; one piece of newspaper, *Globe and Mail*, dated May 9, 1975, blood-stained."

With the blood-soaked wrappings removed, we were able to see that the deceased had been a woman.

Herm: "Female, white, late forties, wearing a dark blue sleeveless sweater."

The woman had suffered a horrendous beating at the hands of someone who had utterly destroyed her emaciated body. The brute had pounded her to a pulp, and then went one better by disemboweling her and severing her legs from her torso at the hips. Her hands and arms were badly bruised; in the initial stages of what was surely a torrential battering, she must have tried to defend herself. But this had been a frail woman whose injuries were so extensive that Herm and I doubted strongly she could have put up much of a defence.

I couldn't help but wonder, as I knelt by her pitiful remains, where God's love goes sometimes. I looked up at Herm and shook my head in complete dismay. "Sweet mother of Jesus! I've never seen anything as bad as this," I said.

As partners, we had stood side by side over the bodies of more than fifty murder victims. And though each of them was tragic, what we were witnessing this morning threatened to upset our mental equilibrium.

Herm tossed out a lifeline. "Here," he said, "grab the end of this

to him that Smoke could not have been the killer; he obviously didn't know that his wife had been cut in half. That horror awaited him.

After talking to Smoke, Wayne briefed Herm and me: "Smoke says he doesn't know The Dude's real name."

"Where does he live?" I asked.

"Ground floor apartment at Church and Gloucester, southwest corner."

I sent George Barrett and three other officers there to see what they could find out.

Barely a quarter of an hour had passed when I got a call from George: "We got inside. Somebody's tried to wash the place down."

"Did they do a good job?" I asked.

"Wouldn't want whoever did it cleaning my house. No, there's no doubt we've got a murder scene here. There's evidence of blood, and lots of it, in all three rooms. You coming over?"

"Be right there."

Within minutes, Herm and I were at The Dude's apartment.

We entered the building from Church Street, walking down a dark, twenty-foot hallway with chest-high wainscoting made of one-inch-square white marble tiles like those found in old-fashioned public toilets.

At the apartment door was a uniformed man wearing an expression of utter misery. We knew why when we closed to within ten feet of him. The stench of decomposing flesh laced with the acrid sting of disinfectant hit us like a fist in the stomach.

I asked the officer, "You gonna be okay?"

"Pretty sure, Sarge, yeah."

"Well, if you think you're gonna toss your cookies, try to do it outside."

"What about you, Bill?" Herm teased. "Where you gonna toss your cookies?"

"In your hat, you goofy, lop-eared herring choker!"

The young officer managed a weak chuckle, then, all pretence gone, scrambled out to the street.

Inside the apartment we found George Barrett taking photographs in the bathroom, where some clothing and a bedsheet identical to the one in which the woman's torso had been wrapped were soaking in the tub.

Herm: "Looks familiar."

George: "Yeah, they match. Take a look at that bundle buggy in the hall."

I had already walked into the hall and was examining it. I called to Herm, "It's got blood on the wheels, and some on the side. He must have moved her in it."

George: "There's more. Check out the kitchen counter and the stove."

This turned up the most shocking detail of all: the stomach-turning stench that had greeted us was emanating from a green bowl on the counter and from a stainless steel pot on the stove. Both vessels contained raw flesh unlike any to be found in the supermarket, and it was rapidly decomposing. It would seem that after murdering her and hacking her body to pieces, Margaret Fraser's killer had committed cannibalism.

A knock sounded on the door. It was the young uniformed officer with a message that we were due at the morgue to witness the postmortem. We left George and the other Ident officers to protect the scene and to photograph and gather evidence – especially a number of knives and a saw found in the kitchen.

Before we left, Herm detailed uniformed officer Danny McLean to discover the true identity of The Dude. After some effort, he was able to locate and interview the landlord of the suspect's building. He learned that the man we were looking for was named Johnnie Bolden, and that he was a newly hired labourer at Ontario Hydro's Pickering generating station. We checked there and learned that he hadn't shown up for work that day. Believing he was lurking about somewhere close by, we assigned a number of officers the time-consuming but wholly necessary task of knocking on doors in the area, in an attempt to locate him.

At about 4:20 that afternoon, as George and two scientists from the crime lab were collecting blood samples in the apartment, another Ident officer, Ron Grumeth, who was lifting fingerprints, looked out the front room window and saw a tall black man matching Bolden's description watching the apartment from the gas station lot across the street. Together with Danny McLean and another uniformed man named John Ladd, the two Ident men left the crime lab scientists and hustled out the front door and across the street. When he saw the police officers coming, the man wheeled about and started walking quickly up Church Street.

Danny McLean was in the lead, and as he crossed the gas station lot, one of the mechanics pointed at the man and nodded, indicating to McLean that this was the one we were looking for. McLean, a giant as well at over six-foot-five, closed the gap between himself and Bolden. Now, just two paces behind him, the officer could hear the man's laboured breathing and see the sweat glistening on his massive neck.

"If he turns on me now," thought McLean, who had neither unholstered his revolver nor taken out his night stick, "I've got one chance to deck him before he grabs me." McLean took two more paces, then came to a sudden halt, his size fourteen boots hammering the pavement as if he were on the parade square.

"Not another step!" he commanded.

Bolden froze.

"Turn around and look at me," McLean commanded.

For the briefest of moments, Bolden hesitated.

"*Now!*"

Slowly, Bolden turned around to face the officer.

"What's your name?"

"My name, Mr. Police Officer, would be *Mister* Johnnie Bolden."

"Well, *Mister* Bolden, you're under arrest for murder."

"Murder?"

"Of Margaret Fraser. You're not obliged to say anything in answer to the charge unless you wish to do so, but whatever you say will be taken down in writing and may be given in evidence."

Bolden said nothing.

McLean and Ladd handcuffed him – but not without some difficulty because his wrists were so large – and drove him to the 52 Division detective office, where, within a very short time, Herm Lowe and I arrived to question him.

He had been taken to a small, windowless interview room on the third floor of the police station, where he remained in the custody of McLean and Ladd. When Herm and I came through the door, we asked Danny to remove the handcuffs from Bolden's wrists, standard procedure whenever we questioned anybody.

The big man was sweating profusely. His spittle had formed frothy white brackets at the corners of his mouth. He had apparently drunk heavily that day – in fact, the entire weekend – and the yeasty tang of second-hand booze filled the tiny room. When he stood up to allow McLean to unlock the handcuffs, I appreciated for the first time how overpowering and menacing the man truly was. His hands were half again as thick and wide as my own. His broad head, with its close-cropped hair, was easily the size of a soccer ball. The massive vault of his chest heaved with every breath. And his arms, the size of a smaller man's legs, looked strong enough to hoist Herm and me off our feet and dash our heads together with one fatal, skull-splitting clap.

We began to question Bolden, and it was one of the most bizarre interrogations of my career. To begin with, Bolden fancied that he was extremely well versed in matters of jurisprudence and told us he was not at all impressed by our command of the law – this because we had offered to help him contact a lawyer. He assured us that we were going about things all wrong. The court, he said, would be his advocate and straighten out the whole thing, we'd soon see. He then began a rambling tirade during which he sometimes spoke to an unseen person. After about fifteen minutes, he fell silent.

Just then one of the uniformed lads knocked on the interview room door and entered with a couple of hamburgers for Herm and me. Bolden had declined our offer to buy him something to eat. I removed the wrapping from my hamburger and was about to take a bite when Herm looked at Bolden (who was sitting right beside me, no more than three feet away) and said, "Stand up for a minute and drop your drawers."

"What?"

The big man seemed alarmed.

"You heard me, drop your drawers!"

Which Bolden did.

"What's that?" demanded Herm, indicating a broad red stain on the front of the man's underwear.

"Well, what does it look like to you, Mister Police Officer?"

"It looks like blood."

"Well, if it looks like blood to you, Mister Police Officer, then I guess it's blood."

"And what's that?" asked Herm, pointing at a small shred of pink matter stuck to Bolden's underwear.

"What does it look like to you, Mister Police Officer?"

"It looks like flesh!"

"Well, if it looks like flesh to you, Mister Police Officer, then I guess Mister Johnnie Bolden better get himself a good lawyer!"

I plunked the hamburger back in its wrapping and shoved it to the far side of the desk towards Herm, who returned my murderous stare with a "whaddid I do?" look.

We seized and bagged every piece of clothing Bolden was wearing right then and there, and got something else for him to put on from his apartment.

There was no point in continuing the interrogation, so we took him back to Headquarters for fingerprinting and mug shots. Though he didn't act up, it was a very nervous Ident officer who grasped Bolden's bear-sized paws and dabbed each finger, thumb, and palm in black ink before rolling out its impression on the identification form. His hands were so big that their impressions exceeded the margins of the paper.

When Ident was finished with him, we took the unusual, though not unprecedented, step of having him examined by a psychiatrist, who confirmed in a preliminary way what every officer attached to this investigation had, over the past several hours, come to believe: Johnnie Bolden was a desperately sick and dangerously violent human being who posed a serious threat to the safety of everybody around him – particularly women. We locked him up to await a pre-trial hearing that would formally determine his mental state.

The interview room was stifling. Herm and I knew by the expression of misery on the woman's face that she'd had about enough of our questions. It was time to sum up and turn her loose.

"You've told us that you saw The Dude carry a big cardboard box across Church Street, that he made you clean up his apartment, that he even paid you and Jackie twenty dollars each. Is that right?"

"I said it, didn't I?" she said irritably.

"Yes, you said it. Just one more question: Can you tell my partner and me what happened this afternoon?"

That did it. She snapped.

"I been through this a dozen times already! I told them two stupid harness bulls who were passin' my place in the cruiser, I told their dumb-ass sergeant, I told that policewoman who kept tryin' to calm me down, I told everybody and his friggin' dog, and now you want me to tell you all over again!"

She convulsed into ragged sobs.

"You want another coffee?" Herm asked.

"No, I don't want another fuckin' coffee. I want to get outa this place and have a beer!"

We waited until she settled down. She took a couple of deep pulls on her cigarette, shook her head in resignation, and finished her story.

"Like I told them other coppers, I decided to wash some clothes but I didn't want to go downstairs 'cause of all that's happened. I just didn't want to be by myself. So I told Jackie to come downstairs with me, and that's when I seen it."

"What did you see?"

"The bag. The green garbage bag with the bone stickin' out of it. We went down to the basement and opened the door that takes you up a few steps to the sidewalk. Somebody had tucked the bag under the steps."

"What did you do then?" Herm asked.

"I started screamin' and Jackie tried to shut me up, but I couldn't stop. I just couldn't . . ."

"Is that when Jackie ran out onto the street and flagged down the passing police car?"

All she could do was nod. She had no more words left.

Margaret Fraser's legs had been found. The pathologist matched them with her torso. In a few days, her body would be released to Noah Smoke.

As we had so many times before, Herm and I worked round the clock on this investigation. By the time we'd finished all the paperwork, and had written our report to the chief, it was about five o'clock Wednesday morning. To make matters worse, we both were due in court at ten o'clock that morning to give evidence in another murder trial.

Both of us were running on adrenaline. It was too late to drive home and grab some sleep, and too early to wake up our families, so we wound up sitting in the Devon Restaurant, across the street from Bolden's apartment, having a coffee and a smoke.

Though Herm and I had investigated scores of homicides, this one had shaken both of us badly. We were numb as we sat in the booth looking out the window at a couple of old cars parked by the curb, rusted four-door sedans with kids' toys and storybooks strewn across their back window ledges – our kids' toys, his and mine.

"If I were still in uniform," I said with a yawn, "I'd probably figure those two old clunkers were unsafe and yank the plates off them."

"I know what you mean," Herm chuckled. "I'm afraid I'll get pulled over every time I drive into the office."

Herm and his wife had three kids, and Jean and I had five. There was never any extra money in either of our households for things like new cars or dinners in fancy restaurants. We were always being ribbed about the rusty old sleds we drove by the single guys on the job who had no one to spend their paycheques on but themselves.

For a few minutes, neither of us spoke. Finally Herm asked, "How could *anybody* do what he did to that woman?"

"I've been trying to figure that out myself," I said.

"What the hell are we doing in this job? It's insane!" Herm shook his head.

"I've been trying to figure that out too. But I can't."

As we got up to leave, Herm said, "I'm thinking of getting the car painted with my next overtime cheque. Know anybody who'll give me a deal?"

"I'll ask around."

"Thanks."

"See you in court."

Johnnie Bolden was found unfit to stand trial. Eventually, he was sent back to Dannemora. I heard that he died quietly in his sleep some years later.

3

The Angel Dust Murder

*W*hen I was nineteen years old I went to sea, and all the world opened up to me. I sought adventure and found it. And after two years in the Merchant Navy, I joined the Bermuda Police. The spring of 1954 held for me nothing but limitless promise. With everything to live for, I was as happy and hopeful a twenty-one-year-old as ever there was. Today, I suppose I'm no different than lots of other people who, as they grow older, reminisce about their youth, when everything seemed possible. Over the years, my wife and I have watched while each of our five children stood expectantly on the threshold of his or her future. Mingled with their happiness and excitement, however, has been the sad reminder of one young man for whom the promise of the springtime of his life never was fulfilled. In all this time, I have not forgotten him, or his family, or that spring day in 1978 when their world came crashing down.

Herm Lowe and I were in our office at Headquarters when the call came through of a shooting at a Vaughan Road appliance store. We headed right out and were on the scene fifteen minutes later.

Sergeant Arley MacDonald met us at the front door of the store.

"What've we got?" I asked.

"A young fellow's been shot several times. The body's at the back of the store."

"Anything else?" asked Herm.

"A couple of our boys found a guy downstairs in the basement when they were searching the place," said Arley.

"What's he got to say?" I asked.

Arley shook his head. "Not much. He's scared shitless."

"What was he doing here?" Herm wanted to know.

"He says he was working on the furnace," responded Arley. "He also told us he heard a commotion upstairs here, but thought somebody was just fooling around. Do you want to talk to him now?"

I shook my head. "He's not going anywhere. Just in case he turns out to be our man, make sure nobody goes near him except the two officers who are with him."

Herm and I walked past MacDonald to the back of the store, where the body of a young man lay face-down with arms and legs outstretched. On the back of his left shoulder, there was a puncture hole from which blood had oozed, and above which there was gunpowder residue. There were deep lacerations on both hands, and on his face were a second bullet hole and powder residue below the left cheekbone. When we moved his body, we found another wound on his left side. The driver's licence in his wallet identified him as twenty-one-year-old Russell Rogers.

One of the uniformed men guarding the body told us the victim had been discovered by a customer. She had been so terrified by what she saw that she couldn't think or act coherently for several minutes afterwards – a common and understandable reaction experienced by many people who are thrust without warning into a situation that is too horrible to comprehend.

It's important to realize that police officers aren't immune to horror themselves. In my time, I've seen some pretty tough coppers go to pieces when suddenly confronted by a tragic or horrifying spectacle. But since the public expects the police to keep their heads in difficult situations (and rightly so), coppers seldom forgive themselves, or each other, when their composure breaks down.

Later that afternoon, the woman would compose herself sufficiently to give Arley MacDonald and his partner, Ron Short, a clear account of the events that led up to her discovery of the body. She told them she had moved into an apartment on Vaughan Road a day or two before, and had come into the store intending to buy an iron. When no one met her near the front of the store, she began to wander slowly around, glancing at various appliances, until she found herself near the back. It was then that her eyes fell on the body of a young man and the pool of blood that had spread out on the floor around his head.

For a moment she froze, unable to utter a sound, unwilling to take her eyes off him, uncertain of what to do next.

Flight. She must get out of there!

The woman turned away, but could not make her legs run. She could not force them to carry her screaming to the street. What a blessed relief it would have been to her at that moment if she had been able to explode onto the sidewalk and rage "Bloody murder!" at the top of her lungs. But she could not utter a sound. She was seized by a desperate and constricting panic that compelled her to walk slowly and noiselessly the entire length of the store, without looking back, and out the front door.

For several minutes, she wandered the neighbourhood in a daze before phoning the police. Eventually she summoned the courage to approach one of the half-dozen uniformed officers who began to gather outside the building in response to her call. She told him what she had seen, and gave him her name and address, but not her phone number, because the telephone company had not yet installed her phone.

She walked slowly across the road to her building and took the elevator to her apartment on the thirteenth floor, where she sat, as if in a trance, in the middle of her unfurnished living room.

An hour passed. Gradually, the full horror of what she had seen filled her small apartment like dense smoke. She buried her face in her hands and wept.

At about the time the woman identified herself to the uniformed police officer outside the appliance store, officers inside were aware they were dealing with a homicide. It was then that Constables Joe Morrison (the first officer on the scene) and Al Iannuccelli began to search the building.

In the basement, they had opened the large steel-clad door to the furnace room to discover a man wearing dirty coveralls standing inside. Iannuccelli levelled his revolver at the man and ordered him to walk slowly out of the room. He told the man to lean with his hands above his head against the wall and, while Morrison looked on, Iannuccelli searched him. As he was being searched, the man said, "Don't tell me what I thought happened really happened!"

When Iannuccelli asked the man what he meant, he replied, "I heard somebody say, 'Don't kill me! Don't kill me!' Then I heard some bangs. I thought it was a starter's pistol. I thought they were fooling around."

The man told the officers he had come to the store to perform scheduled maintenance on the furnace, and had been in the process of vacuuming the air ducts when they discovered him.

Herm and I went over the repairman's story with the two officers, then instructed them to take him to the 13 Division police station near Eglinton Avenue and Dufferin Street so that he could provide us with a witness statement. Before taking the man to the station, we had Iannuccelli search the service truck, the man's tool case, a box of soot that he'd removed from the furnace and air ducts, and the vacuum cleaner that he had used. The officer found nothing.

At the station, the repairman would repeat his account of what had happened while he was busy cleaning the furnace. Upon reflection, he believed it had been Russell who had cried out, "Don't kill me! Please don't kill me!" It was then that he had heard what sounded like a loud *crack!*, followed by running feet on the hardwood floor, then three or four more loud *cracks*, followed by the sound of footsteps running, then staggering, then running again, towards the front door. A buzzer had then sounded, indicating that someone had left the store. Believing that what he'd heard was nothing more than boyish horseplay, the repairman had returned to his work, while upstairs, the life gushed from Russell's body, and in a matter of seconds he was dead.

Moments after the repairman had been discovered by Morrison and Iannuccelli – about 1:50 p.m. – Stephen and Patricia Rogers arrived at the store. Something was dreadfully wrong. There were police cars and police officers everywhere. They opened the front door and entered. At the back of the store, they could see their son lying on the floor facedown in a pool of blood. A number of police officers stood above him talking in low voices to two ambulance attendants. A few feet away other officers glanced around the store and made notations in their books.

Ominously, none of them seemed to be in a hurry.

Patricia began to cry hysterically and was comforted by Stephen, who was himself barely able to maintain control. Together, they started to walk towards Russell's body, but were prevented for their own sake from going any further by the uniformed officer who'd been assigned to guard the front entrance. How they must have wanted to run to their son, to hold him in their arms, to wipe away the blood that covered his face and matted his hair, and to plead with him to tell them, "What happened here, Russell? What went wrong? Why can't you get up?"

While the officer who blocked their way was guided by compassion, he was also bound by the cold and completely necessary practicalities imposed by a serious criminal investigation, which dictate that a crime scene must, at all costs, be preserved. Thus, Stephen and Patricia were prohibited from doing what any loving parents would want and need to do. Instead, they were escorted to the basement of the store and asked to wait until Herm and I arrived.

Seldom had I seen such appalling anguish and despair. As Herm and I approached them, I extended my hand to the father and I said, "Mr. and Mrs. Rogers, my name is Detective Sergeant William McCormack, and this is Sergeant Herm Lowe. Please accept our deepest sympathy on the death of your son."

At first neither parent was able to speak, so deep was their grief. We sat down with them and after waiting a few moments for them to compose themselves, began the heart-wrenching and delicate task of interviewing them.

They told us their son had been a twenty-one-year-old business administration student who was about to graduate from Ryerson. He'd been a popular and handsome young guy with stylishly long hair and a beard, the second eldest of their six well-loved children. Russell's parents had been preparing him to manage the family-owned appliance store, at Vaughan Road and St. Clair Avenue, ever since he was old enough to peek over the countertop.

The boy had come to know and like the business almost as much as his father did. His folks recognized this and trusted him with the store while, just a few weeks before in April, they had taken a much deserved vacation in the islands.

The responsibility for running things in their absence had not been granted lightly. Stephen Rogers had worked in the store since his arrival in Canada from Barbados in 1954, at the age of eighteen. He put in long, hard hours until he was able to buy the business from its previous owner in 1968. Over the years, Patricia and the children – three girls and three boys – worked side by side with him to build it up. Ten years later, the family's determination and hard work began to pay off. They were known in the neighbourhood as solid, trustworthy people, and they had a growing clientele. More importantly to Stephen and Patricia, their children were happy and healthy, each of them a source of deep pride.

When Russell's parents returned from their vacation, they found the business humming like a well-tuned engine. Their trust in him had been warranted.

Today was May 2. Russell had opened the store while his parents, who had worked late the night before, took care of errands close to their Thornhill home, ten miles away. Around noon, Russell telephoned his dad to remind him that he had a dentist's appointment later that afternoon, and to ensure that his parents would arrive at the store in time for him to nip home and grab a shower.

That was the last time Stephen would hear his son's voice.

We would have other questions for Mr. and Mrs. Rogers, but they could wait. Neither one of them was in a condition to continue the interview or to drive, so we arranged to have a cruiser take them home.

After we had made our observations of the scene, the coroner had made a legal pronouncement of death, and photographs had been taken by Ident, the boy's body was removed to the morgue so that the pathologist could conduct a postmortem examination to establish the cause of death. While the cause of death in this case might have been manifestly obvious even to an untrained eye, it was not a finding we, as homicide investigators, were empowered, or medically trained, to make. Quite properly, that determination is the responsibility of the pathologist. For without the sworn testimony of a bona fide medical practitioner, specializing in pathology, as to the cause of death, we would never convict anyone of this crime. Indeed, such evidence is essential to the prosecution in *virtually* every homicide case.

Later that day, Russell's body was formally identified by his uncle Charles to Homicide Squad members Wally Tyrrell and Julian Fantino. The identification took place at the Coroner's building at 26 Grenville Street, and was duly witnessed by the Coroner's Clerk, Jay Sonshine. The postmortem was conducted by Dr. Francis MacDonald.

MacDonald was known for the speed and precision with which he conducted postmortems. He had performed many thousands of them in the course of his long career, which included a lengthy stint in Africa. During the 1950s, in the wake of the bloody violence that attended Kenya's Mau Mau uprising, he worked as a technical advisor for Canada's Department of External Affairs, and later taught and performed forensic medicine at the University of East Africa. He concluded that the bullet wound to Russell's face would not have killed him; nor would a bullet wound found on the right side of his chest, nor even the one that went through his back and pierced his kidney. The ragged lacerations on both of his hands were caused by a single bullet that struck when the boy had raised them in a pitiable attempt to defend himself. In fact, it was the bullet that entered his chest below the rib cage and travelled through the left lung, aorta, and right lung that caused the massive haemorrhaging that killed Russell. He'd bled to death very quickly – the single scant mercy in the entire brutal business.

All this Herm and I were told by Wally Tyrrell and Julian Fantino, just back from the morgue, as the four of us stood drinking coffee from paper cups outside the store. Tyrrell, an intense and methodical investigator not given to swearing, was the senior partner and did most of the talking. He did not describe Russell's injuries in the precise, clinical language of a pathologist, though he certainly could have because he, among all of us on the squad, loved the science involved in post-mortems and was able to converse knowledgeably on that level with the pathologists who performed them. This time, however, Tyrrell had not been struck by the science but by the savagery of the crime. He used the terse verbal shorthand that is understood by police everywhere, and that pulls no punches.

"This was an execution, Bill," he said. "It wasn't enough for the animal who did this to wound the poor kid – shoot him in the face like that – but when the boy tries to scramble away and hide, the bastard follows him. Now even though he's shot in the face, believe it or not, he still has a chance. So he tries to scramble under a desk at the back of the store, but the prick keeps chasing him. The kid looks up from the floor, sees the guy taking aim again and puts his hands up to protect himself. No matter, the rotten sonofabitch pumps more shots into him. It was one of the two bullets he took in the chest that finally did it. He didn't have a chance."

Tyrrell and Fantino were clearly enraged by what the postmortem had revealed and, as they stood talking to Herm and me, neither had yet regained his composure – though, to an onlooker who did not know these men, they might have seemed quite calm and self-contained. But I knew that beneath the surface they were struggling hard to keep their emotions in check. As they described each wound and the damage it had done, I, too, could feel rage welling up from the pit of my stomach.

Herm summed it up for all of us. "We're going to see this thing through," he vowed. "And when we're done, the bastard who did it is going to jail." In so saying, he had put his finger on the only cure for what was ailing us, the one true antidote – a solution to this senseless murder.

Experienced homicide investigators develop idiosyncratic investigative techniques or methods that they employ time and time again. In every one of the homicide cases I investigated – whether or not the murderer or the motive was known, whether or not the person responsible gave me a confession – my tried-and-true method was to draw an imaginary inner circle around the scene, at the centre of which, figuratively speaking, was a pair of shoes filled by the victim. In each case, I tried, as the saying goes, "to walk a mile in those shoes" in an effort to determine why the person had become a murder victim, and to reconstruct the events that led to the tragedy.

By visualizing an inner circle, I was better able to coordinate the collection of all the evidence associated with each murder, whether physical, documentary, or testimonial. I also operated in the belief that, in the initial stages of every investigation, what is *not* known is as important as what is.

By circumscribing an inner circle, I was also able to ensure that the continuity of evidence was never broken. That's why Russell's parents were not permitted to approach and touch their son – as cruel as that prohibition may have seemed. The moment the first police officer arrived on the scene, the body of Russell Rogers was, in effect, under arrest under the authority of the Coroner's Act. If this law did not exist, the body of a homicide victim could be claimed by anyone, and all manner of mischief could be done by people intent on destroying evidence that might convict them of murder. That's why it is a matter of routine that at each entrance to a crime scene, an officer is posted to deny access to all but the investigators and those who have been assigned to help them.

If one were permitted to read the notebooks of Ralph Styler and Oliver Reilly, the two officers we posted at the front door of the store, one would see a detailed, minute-by-minute account of who entered and who left the scene. A similar examination of the notebooks of Homicide detectives Wally Tyrrell and Julian Fantino would reveal how certain body tissues, blood samples, and bullets, collected by Dr. MacDonald, came into their possession, and how these samples were delivered to the scientists at the Centre of Forensic Sciences, otherwise known as the crime lab. If ever we made an arrest in this case, these officers, the Ident officer who took pictures of the post-mortem and of all the exhibits gathered during its course, the pathologist, the crime lab scientists, and many other witnesses, would be called upon to give evidence. If defence counsel were able to prove a break in continuity, a guilty person might go free.

Beyond the inner circle, I always drew a second, or outer, circle to which I assigned the best field personnel I could find – the veteran officers on loan to the Homicide Squad who did so much of the necessary legwork. Sometimes, due to lack of evidence during the initial stages of a case, I would be obliged to move beyond the inner circle, and to operate primarily in the outer circle. Whenever that happened, I knew I'd lost ground. I'd often feel as though I were grasping at straws and would have to resort to investigative aids such as composite drawings, or, as in this case, door-to-door canvassing and appeals to the news media. In such cases, I moved methodically from the outer circle back through the inner circle until I returned to ground zero, where I would take another walk in the victim's shoes. On my way back to the centre, I would carefully review every detail that we had discovered. Invariably, something would emerge – a previously unseen fact, a new piece of evidence, a different and eye-opening perspective.

And so it went in the case of the Russell Rogers murder: from the centre to the outer circle, then back to the centre and out again.

We ruled out robbery as a motive almost immediately. The brutality of the killing, together with the fact that we found more than one hundred dollars on Russell, and over fifty dollars in the till – apparently untouched – led us to believe there was more to this crime than robbery.

Could it have been revenge? To find out if Russell or anyone in his family had enemies, we interviewed a long list of people who drew a composite picture of a family who was well liked, even loved, by virtually everyone who knew them. In fact, Stephen Rogers had been known to have extended credit to people in the neighbourhood who were going through lean times. There were no hidden scandals, no scores to settle – nothing that pointed to revenge as a motive.

Was Russell Rogers the victim of a failed extortion attempt on his father? The only way to discover if somebody had been trying to shake down Stephen Rogers was to question him. Since he found it too painful to return to the store, we agreed to meet him at a restaurant on St. Clair Avenue. Despite his profound grief, Stephen was determined to help us find his son's murderer, and was prepared to do whatever it took to accomplish that – even if it meant submitting to a line of questioning that could only have worsened his suffering. It was a long conversation, but in the course of it, we asked the questions that needed to be asked. He answered every one of them to our complete satisfaction:

"Did you welch on a gambling debt?"

"I don't gamble."

"Do you owe money to a loan shark?"

"Absolutely not."

"Is anybody blackmailing you, Stephen?"

"What for? Why would anybody want to do that?"

Clearly, extortion wasn't the motive.

Our conversation with Stephen Rogers did turn up one interesting piece of information, though. During the past year, a man (who needn't be identified here) had convinced Stephen that he could sell some slow-moving stock at a significant discount. Happy to get the old stock off the floor, even if it meant losing a bit of money, he'd trusted the man to do what he'd promised. In the end, however, the con man had fleeced Stephen out of a significant amount of money. Even though he could have complained to the police, who would have charged the man criminally, Stephen had let the matter drop.

Was there a connection between the con man and Russell's death?

The crook wasn't hard to find. When we paid him a visit, he admitted to scamming Stephen, to say nothing of a lot of other people, too. But when he found out we were investigating the murder of Russell Rogers – a boy he had grown genuinely fond of, even though he was cheating his father – he vowed he'd do everything in his power to help us catch the killer. And he was as good as his word – if one can say that about a con man. He assumed a personal vendetta against whoever had killed the boy, and for the next several days, he prowled every bar, pool hall, and eatery where hoods hung out, in search of information to feed us. He gave us a number of leads, too. Sadly, none of them paid off.

Some people sneer at the notion of honour among thieves, but I've been helped too often by people I'd never introduce to my mother to believe all criminals are bad to the core. In some ways, most rounders are just like the rest of us: treat them like human beings, and they often return the favour.

This case brought out the best in the team we'd assembled to help us with the investigation, too. They matched Herm and me hour for hour, often working double shifts, or even round the clock. A number of the officers from 13 Division, the area where the shooting took place, refused to book off duty or to claim overtime. The killing of such an innocent young man, with everything to live for, obviously stuck in their collective craw. Nothing would do but to find the person responsible and put him in jail.

And so, as the days passed, robbery, revenge, and extortion were, in turn, ruled out as potential motives. And yet, the multiple bullet wounds told us that the gunman had been determined to end Russell Rogers's life. The bullets that struck him were fired from extremely close range – some of them from just a few inches away. The first struck him as he stood by the counter in the middle of the store, seconds after he had pleaded with the attacker not to kill him. After the first shot, Russell had scrambled to the back of the store, where he was pursued by the gunman, who then emptied the revolver into his prone body before running from the store.

As soon as one of the slugs that had been retrieved from Russell's body was turned over to Finn Nielsen, a crime lab ballistics specialist, he called me to say, "Bill, I haven't done any tests yet, but I'm going to tell you right now that it was fired by a turn-of-the-century Ivor Johnson." He would later be proven right.

Our observations at the scene, the physical evidence we had collected, the postmortem examination conducted by Dr. MacDonald, and the repairman's statement all tallied. Together, they added up to a wanton, cold-blooded execution. If not robbery, revenge, or extortion, why had Russell Rogers been killed in such a brutal manner?

The break we needed came in the form of a telephone call, about two weeks after the murder, from an extremely nervous municipal employee of my acquaintance, who offered information in exchange for anonymity. He asked if we could meet for a coffee to talk over something that had struck him as suspicious. Maybe it was nothing, he said, but I'd have to judge for myself.

We agreed to meet at a hamburger joint on the Danforth. The restaurant was at the opposite end of the city from where he lived, and it wasn't hard to figure out why he'd seemed so skittish on the phone. Sure enough, he admitted he was in the middle of an affair. If his wife ever found out, their marriage would be over. He asked me for assurances that his name would never be connected with the investigation. When I promised I wouldn't reveal his secret, he told me his girlfriend had become acquainted with a woman who had recently moved into an apartment near the Don Valley with a real badass named Danny, who was well known to the police. According to my informant's girlfriend, the woman was extremely frightened. The day of Russell Rogers's murder, she had walked into the living room of the apartment to find Danny watching a television news report of the incident. She noticed he was very agitated, and when she asked him what was wrong, he angrily told her he didn't want to talk about it. She asked if it had anything to do with the news report. Turning off the television, he warned her never to mention it again.

A check with Central Records turned up a small-time hood with a history of violent crime named Danny S___. We found out that he and his girlfriend lived on York Mills Road near the Don Valley. We didn't want to try to arrest him inside the apartment; that posed too much of a risk. If he had a gun and panicked, we could end up in a shootout. We decided to bide our time and wait until we could take him down in the open, when he went to his car. That way, we could limit the risks.

A little after noon on May 17, we assembled an arrest team composed of men who worked the old clothes detail at 13 Division and members of the Emergency Task Force. All that long afternoon, they staked out Danny's aging yellow Oldsmobile convertible, which sat in the tenant parking lot of his apartment building.

At quarter after six, Danny S___ and his girlfriend walked out of the apartment building and across the parking lot. She was a few paces ahead of him, and took a seat on the passenger side of the car. Just as he was about to climb in behind the wheel, the arrest team nailed him.

"Police! You're under arrest. Hands on top of the car."

"What's this all about? What do you guys want?"

"Shut your yap and put your hands on the car . . . *now!*"

They searched and handcuffed him, then sat him in the back seat of the cruiser for the fifteen-minute trip downtown, during which not a word was spoken. While the arrest team was en route to Headquarters, other officers checked out Danny's car and executed a search warrant on his apartment. Then they brought his girlfriend back to the station for questioning. The entire operation took less than an hour.

It was essential that we get as much information as possible from Danny's girlfriend before we attempted to question him. Herm and I assigned two detectives from Headquarters, Wally Korchuk and Barry Small, to interview her and take a witness statement. At first, she was a reluctant witness. Slowly, however, and with mounting relief, the young woman revealed to the officers everything she knew about Danny and his involvement in the death of Russell Rogers.

She told the officers she'd met him in mid-April, and had left her husband and two small children to move into his apartment on York Mills about three weeks later – just a few days before the murder. Prior to moving in with him, the woman had met some of his friends, among them a heavy drug user named Douglas Parrack, with whom Danny had grown up in Scarborough. When long-time friends of the woman found out she'd been seeing Danny, they warned her he was bad news, that he was a known drug dealer and pimp. They urged her to break off the relationship immediately, but she stubbornly ignored them.

The morning of the murder, Douglas Parrack came to the apartment where Danny and the woman lived. The two men left together, saying they were going "up north" and that they would be gone several hours. Annoyed at not being included in her boyfriend's plans, the young woman left the apartment and took a bus to the home of a friend. She hadn't been at her friend's place for more than five minutes when Danny telephoned to say he was on his way over to pick her up. A few minutes later, he arrived to take her back to their apartment.

In the car, the woman could see that Danny was extremely agitated about something. When she asked where Parrack was, Danny claimed he didn't know, and that Parrack was "crazy." He told her that he never wanted to see him again, and that if he phoned, she was to tell him he wasn't home.

"Did you do something wrong?" she asked.

"No, but Doug did. That's why I don't want to see him again," said Danny.

They drove on in silence until they got to their apartment. For the rest of that afternoon, the woman tried to get Danny to talk about what had happened. When she saw his reaction to the television news report, she knew.

"Did you do that?" she asked.

"No, Doug did. I wasn't even there. That's why I don't want to see him again. If he ever phones here, tell him I'm not home."

The young woman gave Korchuk and Small even more damning evidence against Danny and Parrack, including the gist of a few face-to-face conversations she'd had with Parrack in the past week that only served to convince her further that he was Russell Rogers's murderer, and that her boyfriend was more involved than he had let on. Finally, she claimed Parrack had been blackmailing Danny into taking part in more armed robberies with the threat that he'd kill him or his girl-friend if Danny didn't cooperate. Danny and the woman had decided to try to get the gun back from Parrack, for it had been Danny who'd given it to him in the first place.

With the girl's statement in our hands, Danny was up the creek. He just didn't know it yet. Still, we needed him to implicate Parrack, and it wasn't going to be easy to get him to do that. He had apparently decided not to cooperate. "I'm not telling you guys shit! I've been through the Hold-up Squad, Morality, 52 Old Clothes – you name it! Pound the piss outa me if you want to; I'm not telling you nothing."

"No, I'm not going to pound the piss out of you," I said. "I'm not even going to lay a hand on you. But I'm going to tell you something, and you'd better listen carefully: based on what I've learned tonight, by the time I've finished my investigation, I'm likely going to charge you – *just you* – with first-degree murder. So you've got a choice to make: either you continue to play the tough guy and take this beef all by yourself, or you smarten up and explain to my partner and me exactly what happened."

"Screw you."

I left the interview room and returned moments later with a typewriter. Danny sat across from Herm with his legs outstretched, elaborately feigning nonchalance. I inserted a departmental statement form into the typewriter and began to read aloud:

"Daniel S___, you have been arrested on a charge of first-degree murder. Do you wish to say anything in answer to the charge? You are not obliged to say anything, unless you wish to do so, but whatever you say will be taken down in writing, and may be given in evidence."

Danny's nonchalance suddenly and completely dissolved.

"Wait a minute! You're not really going to – I didn't kill nobody!"

The message had apparently sunk in: he was going down for this; these cops weren't fooling around. He did an about-face and promised to tell us everything, but not in the interview room. He was convinced it was wired for sound, and that the person he'd been covering for might be able to overhear our conversation. So, I asked him if he was hungry, and when he said he was, I suggested that the three of us go out for a bite to eat.

I don't know who was more astonished, Danny or Herm.

"You mean to a restaurant, Bill?"

"Of course to a restaurant! I'm hungry, you're hungry, and Danny here hasn't eaten since noon. Come on!"

Herm couldn't quite believe his ears. In his entire police career, which included a stretch as a Mountie down east, where he was born and raised, this stalwart, meat-and-potatoes policeman, who believed in doing everything by the book, had never heard of such a hare-brained idea. Taking somebody implicated in a murder out for a sandwich, for cryin' out loud – and just when the sonofabitch was about to spill his guts! I'm sure Herm was thinking I must be out of my bloody mind.

But if he was astonished at the idea of taking Danny out to eat, he was damned near apoplectic when we got up to leave, and I said handcuffs wouldn't be necessary. He looked at me as if to say, "If this bugger decides to run, McCormack, you can chase him, and you can write the memo to the chief, too!"

Danny appeared to have read his mind and asked, "What if I take off?"

"You'd be doing me a big favour," I said. "I'd just turn around, take the elevator upstairs, and bang out a warrant for your arrest on a charge of murder. And by tomorrow morning, every copper in Canada would be looking for you."

No police officer had ever treated him like this before. Stymied, he just shrugged his shoulders and followed me out the door, in front of a watchful and obviously peeved Herm Lowe. Together, we walked across Charles Street and into a little diner on Jarvis, just south of Headquarters, where most of the police officers assigned there were known by all the waitresses. One of them, who was particularly chatty, walked over to our table and, after putting a glass of water in front of each of us, stood with her pad open and her pen poised, ready to take our orders. As we skimmed the menus, she greeted Herm and me by our first names, then glanced down at Danny, whom she didn't recognize.

"I don't think I've seen this one before. Who are you?"

Without taking his eyes off the menu he said, "Somebody you don't want to know. Bring me a hamburger."

The waitress blushed in embarrassment, and took the rest of the orders without a word.

Over coffee, Danny said he was ready to talk. I stopped him and cautioned him that it was very likely that I would charge him with being an accessory to murder. He said he understood, then plunged ahead with his story. There was no stopping him now.

He told us Parrack had come to his apartment the day of the murder, and that he'd watched as Parrack downed some pills, which were known on the street as angel dust, a so-called "soft drug" that produces hallucinations and is used as a horse tranquilizer. Danny said he gave Parrack the gun, and that he had driven him to the area of the store, but had stayed in his car, parked on a sidestreet a few blocks away. About five minutes later, Parrack returned to the car and said, "Let's get out of here! I blew his lights out!"

Danny also said he would show us where Douglas Parrack's girlfriend and his mother lived, since he could be found at either address.

My gamble had paid off.

On the short walk to our office from the restaurant, Herm leaned towards me and, out of Danny's hearing, said, "You've got horseshoes up your ass, Bill. You know that, eh?"

Back at our office, we assigned Wayne Cotgrieve and Ed Everson to put Danny in a cruiser (handcuffed this time) and take him to the area of Broadview Avenue and the Danforth so he could point out the home of Douglas Parrack's girlfriend. As soon as the house was identified, members of the Emergency Task Force went in and found Parrack's twenty-year-old girlfriend alone. They brought her back to Headquarters for questioning.

She was a plain, straightforward girl who had grown up in New Brunswick, and was working her way through school in Toronto. She told us she had known Parrack for about five years, but that they were not romantically involved, "just friends." She was familiar with his extreme mood swings, having seen him fly off the handle many times. On one such occasion, he had flown into an incoherent rage in a downtown Toronto bank when a teller had refused to cash his cheque. Through him she had met and taken an instant dislike to Danny S___, whom she described as "wild and aggressive."

She found out that Parrack had a gun a day or so after the murder, when he took her for a walk in a park that flanks the Don River, behind his mother's house. He dug it up out of the ground and handed it to her. It was old and, because he hadn't wrapped it before burying it, very rusty. She cocked the hammer a couple of times and pulled the trigger: *click! click!* After he made her promise she would never tell anyone about the gun, she helped him wrap it in scraps of paper she tore from a notebook she carried, before burying it again and marking the location with a stick.

While she was giving her statement, heavily armed police officers were silently taking up positions around the home of Douglas Parrack's mother. At midnight, they went through the door with their guns drawn. They found him unarmed and sitting on a chesterfield in the living room. Wayne Cotgrieve approached him.

"Douglas Parrack?"

"Yeah."

"You're under arrest. You'll have to come to Headquarters with us for further investigation."

That was all there was to it.

Exactly twenty-eight minutes later, Parrack was sitting in the middle of the Homicide office staring impassively at Herm Lowe and me. What I remember most about my initial encounter with Douglas

Parrack were his eyes. They were the cold-blooded, searching eyes of a killer, completely devoid of remorse – indeed, devoid of emotion of any kind. Here, in front of me, was the reptile who had ended Russell Rogers's life and plunged his family into unspeakable misery.

As I was bound to do, I cautioned him on a charge of first-degree murder. In response, all he said was, "Man, this is something."

"Do you wish to say anything in answer to the charge?"

"Man, I don't know what to say," he shrugged sullenly.

Parrack never confessed, but he eventually pleaded guilty to second-degree murder. At his sentencing hearing, his defence lawyer claimed, and successfully too, that the angel dust he'd taken immediately prior to the murder had impaired his judgement sufficiently to render him incapable of premeditated murder. He went so far as to suggest that Douglas Parrack believed, at the time he was emptying his revolver into Russell Rogers, that he was actually killing a monster. And so, the very drug that had indirectly unleashed such blind, unfeeling savagery upon an innocent boy whom any man would be proud to call his son had provided his murderer with a way out, and a lighter sentence.

He'd be eligible for parole in ten years.

I suspect the niceties of the law were lost on Stephen and Patricia Rogers, as well as on their surviving children, who would forever be deprived of the love and joy that Russell had brought into their lives.

As a police officer, I was compelled to accept such legalistic manoeuvring without complaint, but I didn't have to like it. And though I can't fault Parrack's lawyer for protecting the interests of his client, or the judge for accepting a plea to the lesser charge, I can't help believing that Russell Rogers and his family were denied justice.

After all these years, my heart remains with Stephen and Patricia Rogers. For them, the promise of spring will forever bring pain.

4

*Murder at the
Royal York*

Spring 1976, Denver, Colorado

*H*e was a smallish man, five-foot-six or -seven, who squinted at the world from behind gleaming gold-rimmed glasses.

Though he was dressed in dark blue prison denims, it was obvious that he kept himself well groomed. His sandy collar-length hair was neatly combed, his fingernails manicured. He held his cigarette with a casual lightness between his fingers, not between thumb and forefinger, lit end inwards to the palm, the way most of his fellow inmates in this Colorado prison did.

It was cunning that kept him alive in the joint. He knew how to ingratiate himself to the heavies whom he dreaded and never crossed. With them, he affected a self-deprecating grin and prattled on in his cornpone Kentucky drawl.

Just a good ol' boy.

Fall 1975, Toronto, Ontario

It was still raining when we pulled up outside the Royal York Hotel.

Uniformed officers from 52 Division and 5 District Traffic had already established a security ring around the entire city block on which stood what was then Canada's largest hotel, and were questioning everyone who attempted to get in or out of the building. They had also sealed off Front Street between York and Bay, allowing only police vehicles – which by now numbered more than three dozen – to occupy the broad avenue beyond the hotel's marquee.

Curious onlookers had begun to huddle and trade rumours under the half-dozen awnings that hung above display windows on the hotel's southern wall. They were obliged to guess at what was going on, since none of the tight-lipped police officers standing in their black slickers on point duty would respond to their shouted queries. Seventy yards across the glistening pavement, many more bystanders had begun to congregate beneath the massive stone columns guarding the entrance to Union Station.

Kitty-corner to the Royal York, patrons occupying rooms on the east-facing wall of the now defunct Walker House Hotel, an old dowager whose beauty and reputation had by 1975 long since faded, pulled back the curtains and were gawking, beer bottles in hand, down at the street.

With the arrival of each additional emergency vehicle, the sidewalk spectators craned their necks to get a better look. They offered one another their opinions as to the significance of this or that new development, regardless of how trivial. There had to be a good reason why so many police officers had descended upon the hotel, and why a large van with the words "Emergency Task Force" printed on the side had drawn up at the front door and disgorged several heavily armed policemen wearing bullet-proof vests.

Officers closest to the bystanders overheard their various speculations: that there'd been a robbery, and that the bandits were holed up inside; that one of them had threatened to jump to his death and take a hotel staff member with him; that there'd been a hostage-taking; even that there'd been a bombing.

All guesses, all wrong.

Once inside, Herm Lowe, Jack McBride, Wayne Smith, and I, all from the Homicide Squad, were escorted unnoticed past a crowd of reporters who'd been admitted to the lobby for an impromptu news conference conducted by Chief of Police Harold Adamson, who gave us a perfunctory nod as we skirted the scrum. We were only too glad to have him draw the media flak while we went unobtrusively about our business.

As we passed, I heard Adamson say, "We know one man is dead, and two police officers – one of them a Canadian Pacific Railway police-man attached to this hotel, the other a Metro uniformed man – are seriously wounded. All of them appear to have been shot by the same person. As far as we are able to ascertain, he may still be in the build-ing. That's why we're presently searching it room by room. Now, I'll take some of your questions . . ."

As we stepped into the elevator, which a uniformed PC had been holding for us, Jack asked, "What time you guys got?"

"One-fifty," I said.

From Herm and Wayne: "Same here."

As if on cue, four notebooks were plucked from breast pockets, and pens scribbled, *Thursday, September 18, 1975: 1:50 p.m., arrived Royal York Hotel. Weather: cool, overcast, and raining.*

Before the investigation ended, all of us would assiduously write down hundreds of details, important and unimportant, in small, lined notebooks. They contained each officer's personal record of everything he did, heard, and saw in relation to the case. More often than not, the notes were made on the fly while physical evidence could still be observed, and while events and people's memories of them were fresh. In the course of a lengthy investigation, it is not uncommon for an investigator to fill two, three, or more of these hundred-page, three and a half by five–inch notebooks. Later, at trial, when you're standing in the witness box, these records are your best – sometimes your only – friend.

In Homicide, reliance on observations recorded in notebooks is especially strong. You learn to ignore nothing and to jot down every-thing. You write your way *in*, and you write your way *out* of a crime scene – and for good reason. The last thing you want is for a defence lawyer to ask you a question the answer to which you ought to know but can't recall. To avoid such an embarrassment, some investigators have gone to extraordinary lengths indeed.

One incident, which frequently has been identified with me, actu-ally involved one of my partners, George Thompson, whose attention to detail was legendary. In the middle of a murder trial, George was being cross-examined by a defence lawyer whose every question he had met with an accurate and detailed answer. With mounting frustration, the lawyer tried to break George's stride by asking him a question he was sure would stump him: "And I suppose, Sergeant Thompson, that if I were to ask you the wattage of the bulb that had been inserted into the kitchen light fixture, you'd know the answer to that question, too. Is that correct?"

Casting a self-satisfied glance in the direction of the jury, the lawyer sauntered casually away from the witness box, where George stood, and towards the oak counsel table, pausing briefly to flick a speck from his shiny black gown. When he arrived at the table, he turned again to George. "Sergeant Thompson, did you hear my question?"

With stolid patience, George thumbed through his notebook, until he came to the appropriate page, then said, "Yes, sir. It was a one-hundred-watt bulb." And then, for the sake of precision (or more likely, knowing George, just for the sheer hell of it), he added, "Sylvania . . . frosted."

Totally exasperated, the lawyer slumped to his chair. "I have no further questions, Your Honour."

The elevator stopped at the eighth floor, and we all got off.

Outside Room 8-267, a uniformed man stood guard. Inside, Ident officers George Buffet and Ron Grumeth were taking photographs. We left them to their work, intending to return later, and walked past the room to the east end of the hall, where we turned left into an intersecting hallway. There we met John Garrow, a uniformed constable from 52 Division, who'd been the second Metro police officer on the scene. He was standing a few feet from the blood-soaked body of a young man who was lying face-up in the middle of the hall. He was identified to us as twenty-two-year-old Priyal DeSilva, the hotel's assistant credit manager. He'd been shot in the leg and in the face, and, as the autopsy would later show, had drowned on his own blood.

We learned from Garrow that there were three eyewitnesses to the events that led up to DeSilva's murder. One of them was Anthony Padalino, the hotel's credit manager. While Herm, Jack, and I concentrated on collecting evidence from the hallway where DeSilva had been murdered, we assigned Bill Evans, a detective attached to the Morality Squad, to take a statement from Padalino, who was understandably distraught over the death of his young friend and assistant.

Padalino told Bill that DeSilva had come to his office around noon that day because the guest in Room 8-267, a man who'd checked in under the name of Matheson, had run up a tab of almost four hundred dollars — more than double the hotel's credit limit. Matheson had used a Chargex credit card when he'd registered a few days before. When DeSilva checked with Chargex, he discovered that the card had been stolen. He also checked with Bell Canada and learned that there was no telephone listing in the name of Matheson at the Ottawa address he'd written in the hotel register.

"I'd been out all day, September 17, helping somebody in politics who was running for office drive voters to the polls. She won, and we celebrated 'til about five or six in the morning. I guess I drank a full bottle of champagne in about a ten-hour period.

"I'd planned to take the noon Turbo train to Montreal. I left a message with the switchboard to give me a wake-up call so I'd have enough time to take a shower and eat breakfast . . . Now, I really don't want to say what I was going to do in Montreal, but I was going to make a 'transaction.' Well . . . it was counterfeit money, is what it was. And the people I was going to be dealing with, well . . . I was going to take the gun with me, just for self-defence."

The guy was a fraud, one of hundreds each year who check into good hotels to eat, sleep, drink, and scam local merchants – all on somebody else's plastic. It is such a common occurrence that hotels like the Royal York have developed routine procedures to deal with it. DeSilva was sent to his office to get the master key while Padalino arranged to have a railway policeman meet him outside the room. The people at Chargex, who wanted their credit card back, had already notified Metro Police, and an officer had been dispatched to the hotel.

And so, at 12:35 p.m., while Metro constable Garry Silliker, CP constable Roger Saunders, and Priyal DeSilva waited out of sight a few feet down the hall, Padalino approached Room 8-267.

"I hear a knock on the door, and look out the peephole. And all I see is just one guy wearing a business suit.

"I say, 'Who is it?'

"He says, 'I'm the hotel credit manager, Mr. Matheson, and I need to talk to you.'

"I say, 'I'm not dressed yet. I'm just going to take a shower. Can you come back in about fifteen minutes?'

"I figured he'd leave and I'd take off. It had worked before countless times in countless hotels. As soon as he left, I'd grab my bags and walk down the stairs and I'd be gone, 'cause he don't know what I look like."

Outside in the hall, they waited one . . . two minutes. Then Padalino knocked again. This time more insistently.

"'Okay! Okay! Just a minute.'

"So I open the door, but I leave the chain lock on. All I see is just one guy. My intention was to let him into the room, put the gun on him, tie him up, and get the hell out of there!

"I say, 'Okay. Just a second.'

"I go to my suitcase, get the shells, load the gun, put the rest of the shells in my pocket, hide the gun in my breast pocket, and open the door."

The four men who had been waiting in the hall entered the room single file.

"I'm thinking, 'Oh, my God! What the hell is goin' on?'

"I see the door close, so I says to myself, 'Well, that's all of 'em.'"

Padalino introduced himself and said there seemed to be a problem with Matheson's credit card. Did he have any identification?

"So, on impulse – I mean it's speeding through my mind – I'm gonna tie 'em up. I mean I know I can't shoot four people and get away with it. I figure all of 'em ain't credit managers; some of 'em are plainclothes policemen and one uniformed policeman, and nobody's got his gun drawn or nothin'. I just wanted to tie 'em up and get the hell out of there with my money (a quantity of counterfeit and real cash) *'cause I know I'm goin' to jail, if they open my suitcase, for ten to fifteen years."*

The man smiled pleasantly at Padalino, giving the impression that he was only too happy to clear up this little misunderstanding. Certainly he had identification, right over here on the dresser.

"I say, 'Here's my identification.' And I turn around and pull the gun out like that, and I say, 'Stop! Don't anybody move, and nobody'll get hurt.' Then I see the hotel detective right at the edge of the bathroom door. The uniformed policeman sees I got a gun on him. He's got sense, he raises his hands up. Everybody puts their hands up except the railroad detective. He's divin' into the bathroom. So I run and knock one of 'em over and say, 'Everybody hit the floor!'"

In his statement, CP constable Roger Saunders recalled backing into the bathroom while the gunman ordered everyone to lie on the floor. For one brief moment, he was out of the man's field of vision, and seized the opportunity to go for his gun. But he wasn't fast enough.

"I jump and kick the bathroom door and come back down with the gun, like that. The guy in the bathroom is comin' around with his gun."

Saunders: "I crossed my right hand over towards my left hip, where my gun was in a holster. As I was doing this, the man with the gun was now directly in front of the bathroom door, standing in the narrow hallway, looking directly at me with his gun in both hands, and crouching in the combat position."

"So, I'm in a crouch with my gun cocked and loaded with five shots. I say, 'Please don't move. Drop the gun.' But he keeps on bringing it around until it's almost on me."

Saunders: "I never did make contact with my service revolver. All of a sudden, a shot rang out, and I fell to the bathroom floor, backward to my right."

Constable Silliker: "Then he turned and stepped towards me, aiming the gun at me. I swung to my right and threw my left arm up to protect my face. He fired, and the shot hit me in the left shoulder blade, and knocked me onto the bed."

"One guy runs into me (It was a terrified Priyal DeSilva desperately attempting to escape.) *and I start to run into the hallway. I don't want him getting to the elevator, so I shoot him in the leg. He had no gun in his hand; that's why I shot him in the leg. But I don't want him runnin' down the hall hollerin' mayhem an' murder.*

"And I'm not thinking. Everything's instinct, at this time. There's no plan, no nothin'. I come back into the room, I grab my attaché case, I run back into the hallway. This guy who's shot in the leg, he's runnin' too, and we're about to turn. I'm about halfway down this corridor, and I feel something whiz by me. And I turn around and somebody's shootin' at me! They found the bullet holes in the doorjamb.

"I shot – no aiming – I'm probably forty . . . fifty feet away. I'm not that good of a shot with a .38 snub nose. I just shot to put him down.

"The first shot, they both dropped. The second shot hit the guy I'd shot in the leg, in the head. He died."

Garry Silliker recalled these few frantic seconds differently: "I got up off the bed, drew my service revolver, and went out of the room and ran to the right, though I can't recall why I went to the right. When I reached the north–south hallway, I looked up ahead and saw Mr. DeSilva lying on the floor. There was a maid's cart almost directly beside him.

"The man was at the north end of the hallway and had turned to face me. He raised his gun and pointed it at me. I fell to the floor and took up a position behind the maid's cart. Then I got to my feet and fired three shots at the gunman."

Significantly, Silliker does *not* say the man fired at him, which indicates that the gunman had shot and killed Priyal DeSilva *before* Garry Silliker ran into the north–south hallway. His claim that he returned Silliker's fire was totally false, though, as we were to learn, totally in character. When, as the officer said, the gunman took aim from where he stood at the end of the hall, it was with an empty gun. To his shock, he suddenly realized that he had already spent all five shells. Two of them had struck Priyal DeSilva, the second one in the face, and he was already mortally wounded and lying face-up on the floor when the officer got to him.

All of Silliker's shots missed, and the man fled.

The officer chased him through the stairwell door and down to the seventh floor, where he encountered five hotel maids standing in the doorways of various rooms, screaming. One of them pointed towards an exit door and yelled, "He went through there!"

The officer ran towards the door, opened it, and stood very still, listening.

Not a sound.

Was the gunman waiting in ambush in the stairwell? Had he fled to the floors below? Or had he done the unexpected and doubled back upstairs?

Silliker was beginning to grow weak from loss of blood, which oozed from beneath his left armpit, soaking his shirt. He staggered into one of the rooms and lay on the bed while he dialed the police switchboard, which had already been informed by someone at the hotel that there'd been a shooting. He was put directly through to the communications supervisor, and gave a complete description of the gunman before hanging up and making his way by elevator to the lobby, and then out onto the street, where a waiting ambulance transported him to Toronto General Hospital.

As the gunman rampaged down the stairways and along the halls of the Royal York, Garry Silliker's back-up, Constable John Garrow, stepped out of the elevator on the eighth floor, at the intersection of the east–west and north–south hallways. Leaning up against the wall a few feet away was a man who was holding his right side in obvious pain. As Garrow approached the man, he could see that he was bleeding badly.

Garrow: "He told me he was a railroad police officer, and that he'd been shot at point blank range by a man who had, moments before, fled around the corner. I took the injured man's revolver from him, and went towards the north–south hallway in search of the gunman."

As soon as Garrow turned the corner, he saw a man lying in a pool of blood about twenty feet away, trying to raise his right arm. Believing this was the gunman, Garrow yelled, "Drop the gun!" This he repeated several times. To make matters even more difficult, some of the hotel guests opened their doors to see what was going on. He ordered all of them back inside and warned them to keep their doors closed.

Just as Garrow decided to move in closer, the man's body convulsed, then he lay motionless. The officer checked for a weapon and a pulse, but found neither. He went into one of the rooms and called for more back-up. Then he returned to the injured man he'd found beside the elevator. He told Garrow his name was Saunders, but he was in too much pain to provide a description of the man who'd shot him. Padalino, however, was able to furnish a description, which would match the one given by Garry Silliker. In a few minutes, the hotel was alive with police officers searching for a thirty-year-old white male with sandy-coloured collar-length hair, wearing glasses, a brown sports jacket, blue shirt, beige slacks, and carrying a small, black handgun.

Roger Saunders was also taken to Toronto General, and, like Garry Silliker, would survive his injuries.

"I got on an elevator and put my gun away. I walked through the lobby and out of the hotel to my car, which I drove to the Hyatt Regency, five blocks away. I parked in the Hyatt Regency, ran upstairs, caught a cab. I said, 'I'm in a hurry. My plane leaves in forty-five minutes, I've got to get to the airport. Here's a twenty-dollar tip in advance.'

"He took me to the departures level; I walked upstairs to the arrivals level and caught another cab. I said, 'I just got in from Florida, and I need to go to the Niagara Falls Sheraton Hotel.'"

Cabby Miyazi Tombulon: "I asked him, 'How much do you wish to pay me?' He says, 'Sixty-five dollars, including tip.' I agreed and we left the airport.

"As we approached Niagara Falls, I heard him open his briefcase and shuffle some papers. He said, 'Oh, my God! I can't find the telephone number.' I looked in the rearview mirror and saw him put something in his breast pocket."

"So we stop at the Sheraton Brock, which is right across from the Peace Bridge leading to the United States. I'd planned to walk over it to get the hell out of Canada.

"I said, 'My secretary made the reservation. Would you watch my briefcase while I check at the reception desk? I'm not sure if this is the right hotel.' In the meantime, I'd opened my briefcase and taken out my money and the papers I needed.

"I walked in the front door and immediately walked around and out the back door. Then I walked over the Peace Bridge to get to the United States. I had my gun in my belt.

"The border guard asked me, 'What nationality are you, sir?'

"I said, 'I'm a U.S. citizen.'

"He asked, 'Do you have anything to declare, coming in?'

"It was still sprinkling, so I smiled and said, 'Nothin' but some of this damned Canadian rain. And I'd sure like to get home.'

"He said, 'Well then, come on home, son!'"

America would soon regret this prodigal's return.

When all of the measurements and appropriate photographs had been taken, and we had finished collecting spent bullets and other physical evidence from the hallway where Priyal DeSilva was murdered, we went back to room 8-267, where the initial shootings took place – the room that had, for the past few days, been occupied by the man who'd assumed the identity of Mr. Matheson of Ottawa. George Buffet, who had already photographed the room and its contents, dusted for finger-prints and found one on a bottle of cologne that had been sitting on the bathroom counter.

Hanging in the closet, we found tailor-made slacks, sports jackets, and suits, bearing labels from Toronto, New York, and San José – one of which read, "Custom Tailored for R. Embry." Neatly packed in expensive luggage, we found custom-made shirts, a number of silk ties, and keys for six other Canadian hotels. On the closet floor were styl-ish brown leather loafers, size six and a half.

"I'd made plans to go to Canada, 'cause I already had some credit cards. I was gonna go up there for two months and get me a real good, fancy wardrobe, and get enough money to buy a new car."

In the breast pocket of a blue suit jacket we found two traffic tickets – one issued in July by the Ontario Provincial Police, and the other in August by the Quebec Provincial Police – both of them charging Roy Allan Embry of Louisville, Kentucky, with exceeding the speed limit in his 1974 Ford Torino, licence ASM 479.

Late in the afternoon, we got word that a cabby had taken a man answering the gunman's description from Toronto International Airport to the Sheraton Brock Hotel in Niagara Falls. It turned out that when the cabby realized that the man had tricked him out of his fare, he called the local police. It didn't take long for them to match the description of the man in the cab with the one we had put out on Telex of the man we were looking for in Toronto.

By that time we had run a check on Roy Allan Embry and discovered that he had a lengthy criminal record in the United States. In Canada, he was wanted for escaping from the Guelph Reformatory, where he had been doing time for theft. His physical description perfectly matched our shooting suspect. It wasn't long before we obtained a photograph of Embry, which, along with photographs of numerous other criminals, was shown to all of the witnesses to the Royal York shootings. Without exception, they picked Embry's photo from all the rest. We issued a Canada-wide warrant for Embry's arrest, and began the search for his Ford Torino.

A day after we issued the alert, Constable Chuck Lawrence was patrolling in the Yorkville area, near Avenue Road and Cumberland Avenue. Between radio calls, he kept a sharp eye out for Embry's car, figuring he may have hidden it far enough away from the Royal York to avoid being immediately associated with it, but close enough to get to in a hurry. It was an educated guess based on the alert young officer's knowledge that "paper hangers" like Embry – criminals who run up big tabs on stolen credit cards and pass worthless cheques – try to leave themselves several escape routes, and have been known to park vehicles that are traceable to them several blocks away from where they ply their dubious trade. Lawrence got out of his police cruiser and began searching the underground parking lots in the neighbourhood on foot.

He guessed right.

In an out-of-the-way corner of the underground garage at the Hyatt Regency Hotel he found the car backed into a poorly lit parking space. Within fifteen minutes, Jim Newsome, another Homicide Squad member, arrived at the hotel to take charge of the car.

At the outset of this investigation, I had assigned Jim the task of collecting all the physical evidence associated with the case: the bullets and spent shell casings found at the Royal York, the body tissues and blood samples collected at the postmortem, and the clothing, partial box of bullets, and papers seized from the gunman's hotel room. He would personally initial, package, and label every one of these articles before turning them over to the crime lab for analysis. Assigning one exhibit officer ensured that the continuity of each piece of evidence could not be broken.

Even though we knew who we were looking for, it was still necessary for us to treat Embry's car with the same care we would any other major crime scene. It promised to yield even more evidence – not only as to his many assumed identities, but as to where he had been and where he might be headed. Newsome had Ident officer George Barrett come to the hotel to photograph the car and dust it for fingerprints. It didn't take long for Barrett to discover that someone had wiped it clean. He had a police tow truck take it to the 1 District Traffic Garage, near the Canadian National Exhibition grounds, where he would examine the car's interior and contents.

Using a special set of keys, Barrett entered the car. He found it lived-in and messy. Matchbooks, empty cigarette packages, and gum wrappers, together with audio cassettes, were strewn on the floor and tucked into creases in the upholstery. In the trunk, Barrett found road maps of Ottawa and a suitcase. In the glove compartment, he came across an assortment of personal papers – invoices, cash receipts, and the like. These he photocopied then treated with ninhydrin, a chemical that reacts to the body acids that are deposited on paper when it is touched.

The ninhydrin did the trick: Barrett raised and photographed several clearly defined fingerprints, which he compared to those that were contained in Embry's Ontario Provincial Police and RCMP files.

They matched.

From fingerprint evidence alone, we could now tie the Ford Torino to Embry, and thus Embry to his room at the Royal York, where, the day before, George Buffet had lifted his fingerprint from the cologne bottle. Even if he hadn't been eyeballed at the hotel by the police officers he'd shot, or by the terrorized credit manager, Embry's fingerprints established irrefutably his identity as Priyal DeSilva's killer and his presence at the scene. And they would just as surely lead to his conviction – that is, if we could ever get our hands on him.

A few weeks after the shootings, Jack McBride and Wayne Smith flew to Louisville, Kentucky, where, with the help of local police, they tracked down and interviewed a former girlfriend of Embry's who owned a .38 calibre Smith & Wesson revolver. She said the gun had been taken by Embry some weeks before, and she hadn't seen him since.

Throughout October and November I had telephone conversations almost daily with people who were related to, acquainted with, or had been scammed by Roy Allan Embry. I also talked to a lot of American police officers. Everybody I spoke to wanted this guy behind bars, among them an aunt who lived in Denver, Colorado. Two years earlier, her son, Embry's cousin, had been shot to death by an armed robber in an incident not connected to Embry. She understood the trouble Embry was in and the kind of misery he had already caused and might cause again. She wanted him off the street as soon as possible, and agreed to contact me if ever he tried to reach her.

On December 10, she heard from him and phoned me in Toronto.

"The reason I was in Denver was I called my aunt up to borrow two hundred dollars."

She told me Embry had pleaded with her to lend him some money, though he never told her what he intended to do with it.

*"I was planning to get married. I already had a new passport and new iden-
tification, and me and this girl was gettin' married, and we was leaving for
Australia after the first of the year."*

Embry's aunt told him she knew he was on the run, and urged him
to give himself up. But he wouldn't listen to her.

*"I needed that money 'cause I was goin' to Texas to meet her parents. I
already had the boat tickets. We were sailing from New Orleans on January 3
to Australia. We both had passports and I was goin' there to file for landed
immigrant status, and never come back for the rest of my life."*

To stall him long enough to contact me, she agreed to lend him the
money, and to meet him later that evening at the Denver bus station.

As soon as the woman and I completed our conversation, I telephoned
Denver police headquarters to tip them off that a man who was on the
Most Wanted list in both countries could be found later that evening at
their bus station. Then I gave detailed instructions as to how to contact
Embry's aunt so that a plan for capturing him could be devised.

When I reminded the Denver officer to whom I spoke that Roy
Allan Embry was known to be armed and extremely dangerous, and
that he had already killed one man and seriously wounded two others,
he responded in a condescending tone, "Everybody down here is
armed and dangerous."

While other police officers waited in the general vicinity of the bus
station, only two plainclothes detectives were actually sent in to search
for and arrest Embry. When they found him they moved in, but a
struggle ensued, and he broke free. He shot one man to death right
there on the spot and gravely injured the other. A uniformed officer

chased him and shot him down in the middle of the street, putting a bullet in each arm, and one in his left cheek.

"And I turned and looked up at him and I said, 'Why did you shoot me?'"

Three days after Christmas, Jack McBride and I landed in Denver, where we met with local police and the district attorney, on whom we served notice of Canada's intention to extradite Embry should he ever be released from custody.

The next day, we met Roy Allan Embry himself. He was chained to a wall in the prison ward of the Denver General Hospital. I introduced myself and Jack, and explained that we were there investigating the Royal York shootings. I told Embry that although Jack and I had no police powers in the United States, I was obliged to caution him that he was charged with one count of murder and three counts of attempted murder. Then I asked him if he wished to say anything in answer to the charges.

For a moment, Embry said nothing. He took a long drag on his cigarette while he ran his finger down a list of names printed on a large piece of foolscap.

"Your names are on this list as witnesses. I have a good attorney, and he says I shouldn't talk to anyone, including my aunt, who is also listed on this witness sheet."

He took another couple of puffs on his cigarette, then:

"Can I ask you a couple of questions?"

"Go ahead," I said.

"Is there capital punishment up in Canada?"

At that time, only the murder of police officers and prison guards carried the death penalty.

"Not for the murder you're charged with. You're charged with murder punishable by life imprisonment."

"I want to talk to you, but I want to know what my attorney thinks."

At that point, he gave Jack the name and phone number of his lawyer. He left the room and phoned the man while I remained with Embry, who provided me with some non-incriminating details about his life. He was curious about the fate of the Canadian politician he'd campaigned for.

"We kicked around a bit up there, you know. She rides a motorcycle."

Jack came back into the room: "I spoke to your lawyer, and he told me to remind you not to talk to anyone. But, if you want to, it's your right to do so."

For an instant, and only an instant, Roy Allan Embry's thoughts were completely transparent. We could read his mind, and he was clearly thinking, "I can't believe that these two coppers are playing it straight with me! They aren't trying to screw me around."

The fact of the matter was neither Jack nor I gave a damn if he confessed or not. As far as we were concerned, he was bang-up; we had all the evidence we'd ever need to convict him. We left Colorado and headed home. Eleven months later, in a Denver courtroom, Embry pleaded guilty to one count of murder and one count of aggravated assault in connection with the bus station shootings. He was sentenced to thirty-seven years in federal prison.

And it's unlikely that he'll ever get time off for good behaviour. For one thing, he was caught running a highly successful brothel inside the prison and, for another, he had managed for years – and within those same prison walls – to run an elaborate direct mail scam that cost the United States government tens of thousands of dollars.

But if he ever does get out, you can bet the Metropolitan Toronto Homicide Squad will be waiting.

5

Getting Away
with Murder

*S*ometimes even the best efforts of experienced police investigators and forensic scientists aren't enough to uncover the misdeeds of a clever and determined criminal. In such cases, it is often the arrogance of the criminal himself that ultimately trips him up. Gerald Blair was such a criminal. And if he hadn't bragged about getting away with murder, we might never have known it was he who, seven years before, had so brutally taken the life of Olive Revell.

The psychiatric hospital at Penetanguishene sits on several acres of treed parkland that slope gently down to a small inlet off the south-eastern corner of Georgian Bay. Despite the idyllic setting, it is in reality a fortress with high walls, guardhuts, and barred windows. It is composed of a number of aging buildings that house patients and which smell strongly of disinfectant, tobacco smoke, and urine. There, the criminally insane are held in captivity – many of them until they die. On a bone-chilling January morning in 1972, with an icy blizzard howling off the bay, Penetang became the starting point of an investigation into the macabre murder of a Toronto woman in her apartment seven years before.

Jack McBride and I had driven north that day from Toronto to question twenty-eight-year-old Gerald Blair. We wanted to know what he could tell us about a woman by the name of Olive Revell, whose death, followed by a thorough investigation by Metro detectives and forensic scientists, had been listed as an accidental drowning, but which investigators in Brockville suspected was murder.

At the double-gated main entrance to the hospital, where we surrendered our service revolvers, Jack and I were given directions to the building in which Gerald Blair was housed. When we arrived at the building on foot, we were met by Blair's psychiatrist, a flamboyant character who wore a multicoloured bandanna, pirate-style, on his head, and a gigantic hypodermic needle in a holster on his hip, with which, I fervently hoped, he intended only to inject humour into a decidedly humourless place.

We followed the doctor down a long corridor past a bullpen in which were confined a dozen men who prowled ceaselessly from one side of the big cage to the other. Along the same corridor were smaller cells, and in the corners of some, men could be seen cowering. The air was full of dreadful shrieks and rank with the stench of human feces.

The doctor guided Jack and me to a small interview room off one of the corridors on the ward. Some of the more controllable inmates had free access to this room, which was no more than five feet wide and nine feet long and had small, barred windows at both ends. One looked out on the grounds, which the fast falling snow was doing its best to obliterate, and the other allowed numerous inmates who were wandering the hall to take turns gawking and making grotesque faces at us through the smudged glass.

In a few minutes, Blair and the psychiatrist entered the room. I introduced myself and Jack, who offered his hand. Blair ignored the gesture, sat down, and immediately began rolling a cigarette. The psychiatrist left the room and closed the door behind him.

Though Blair was only twenty-eight years old, I was astonished at how much he had aged since a police photograph had been taken of him eight years before. In the picture, he had youthful skin, clear eyes, and thick wavy hair. But the man sitting in front of me passively smoking and spitting loose bits of tobacco on the floor was prematurely bald, and what hair remained was swept back over his ears. There were dark, puffy bags under both eyes and deep creases around his mouth. He looked much older than his years.

After giving Blair the standard police caution, I said, "Gerald, we want to talk to you about something that happened in Toronto about seven years ago to a woman named . . ." I paused as though searching for the woman's name in the pile of papers I had in front of me.

"Olive," he offered, without hesitation.

"That's right, Olive. What can you tell us about her, Gerald?"

In the course of the next three hours, Gerald Blair recalled for us the smallest details about the victim's apartment and the horrible way in which he had sexually attacked and killed her. Blair's confession, together with the original sudden death report and a number of witness statements, helped Jack and me to reconstruct the sex-murder of Olive Revell – a crime that had gone undetected until now.

When they were built in the 1920s, the four-storey yellow brick apartment buildings at 36 and 42 Maitland Street, near Yonge and

Wellesley Streets, offered tenants a respectable and, for the times, reasonably fashionable address.

Joined in the middle, the twin H-shaped buildings are known as "The Maitlands." The roofs of the porticos at each of their front entrances are supported by white Corinthian columns. There are stained-glass panels in most of the windows. The carpeted hallways are generously wide and admit daylight from windows at either end. On each apartment door there used to be a glass knob that looked like a huge brilliant-cut diamond. Over the years, as one by one they broke, the knobs were replaced by drab aluminum handles whose sole redeeming feature was their conformity to modern building codes. When The Maitlands were new, each apartment had its own fireplace that kept out the chill of Toronto's long winters.

In the fall of 1965 only the fireplace mantels remained. Nevertheless, much of the old buildings' charm, most of their glass doorknobs, and all of their respectability were intact. And while they could no longer pretend to be fashionable, The Maitlands could still offer their tenants — mostly retirees whose children and grandchildren lived in the suburbs, or single, middle-aged men and women who worked in the offices nearby — privacy and a solid sense of permanence.

This is where Olive Revell, an attractive forty-nine-year-old legal secretary, lived quietly and contentedly alone. Monday through Friday the trim five-foot-two brunette worked at a small downtown law firm. On weekends, she performed clerical duties for the 48th Highlanders, in which regiment she held the rank of corporal. Sunday mornings she attended St. Andrew's Presbyterian Church at King and Simcoe Streets. On Sunday afternoons she participated in regimental functions, which were frequently held at the York Armouries, before taking

Radko Govedarov killed Trevor Poll and then fled to Los Angeles, where he shot a police officer. Extradited to Canada, he was convicted of Poll's murder but escaped prison, only to be arrested and locked up again.

Russell Rogers, victim of the "Angel Dust Murder" – a son any parent would be proud of.

Some members of the team that worked on the Trevor Poll case. Front row: George Thompson (left), Crown Attorney Norm Matusiak, and me. Back row: Constable Ken Greer (left) and Constable John Booth.

Human tissue found on Johnnie Bolden's underwear exactly matches a wound on Margaret Fraser's horribly battered, dismembered body.

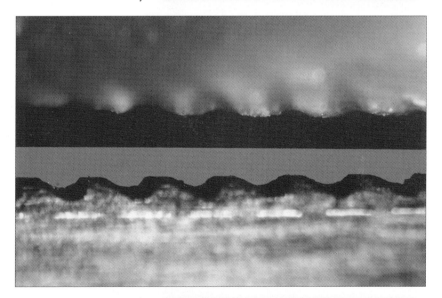

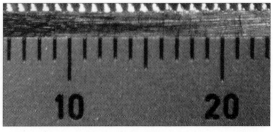

A serrated knife blade is matched with serration on human tissue found on Johnnie Bolden's underwear.

"Mister Johnnie Bolden innocent! Wouldn't even hurt no fly!"

Sgt. Bob Cook pointing to the handsaw found in Johnnie Bolden's kitchen.

The scene in front of the Royal York Hotel moments after Roy Allan Embry shot his way out.

Herm Lowe (left), Jack McBride (right), and I note the position of a slug from one of the bullets fired by Embry at murder victim Priyal DeSilva.

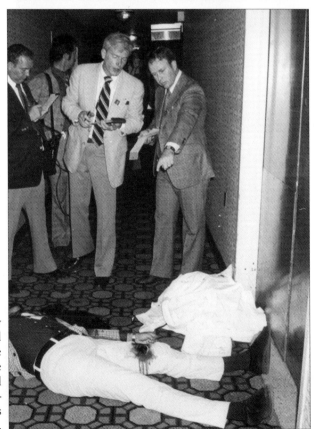

I am flanked by Herm Lowe and Wayne Smith as we stand above the body of Priyal DeSilva in the hallway where he was gunned down.

Gerald Blair as he would have appeared to his victim, Olive Revell, in 1965.

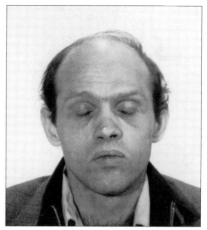

A prematurely aged Gerald Blair as he appeared to Herm Lowe and me when we interviewed him at Penetang in 1972.

As George Thompson and I discovered, there really was "a dead body in St. James Cemetery."

Daniel "Boots" Pearce stole from his uncle the gun that Charlie Walker used to kill Gord Stoddart.

The aftermath of Ryan Kelso's rage. Kelso's former girlfriend, Emily Ward, and her newfound lover, Richard Tucker, lie dead in the bathroom at the end of a hall riddled with shrapnel.

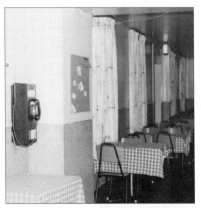

My long shot pays off. Fingerprints lifted by Ident man Dave Rigby from this much used pay phone at Masaryktown Hall led us to Lloyd Blake.

The 9-shot .22 calibre revolver used to kill Gord Stoddart is found at the base of a hydro pole near Markham Road.

Lloyd Blake is escorted into headquarters by Jack McBride and me after giving himself up to Police Cadet David Theriault at 31 Division.

The lonely stretch of Scarborough Golf Club Road where Gord Stoddart was lured to his death.

Chalk mark on the road, where Constable Tony Meyler found mortally wounded cabby Gord Stoddart.

The 1972 Homicide Squad. Front row: Jack Evans (left), Jack Webster, Adolphus Payne, James Noble, Jim Crawford. Middle row: George Thompson (left), Winston Weatherbie, John Leybourne, Sandra C. Morgan, John Mitchell, James Majury, Walter Tyrrell. Back row: William McCormack (left), William Kerr, Frank Barbetta, Mark Dodson, Bernie Nadeau, Jimmy Read, Jack McBride.

the streetcar home, where she would change out of her uniform and have a bite to eat before heading off to her Sunday evening camera club meeting.

In this fashion, Olive Revell routinely boxed the compass of her week.

In 1965, the city was still able to live up to its reputation as "Toronto the Good." Women who worked the afternoon shift in factories around the city, or at the hospitals on University Avenue, waited at streetcar stops at eleven or twelve o'clock at night unaccompanied and unafraid, and nobody thought anything of it. On most city streets, pedestrians walked without fear at any hour. And, just as it was in the majority of older downtown apartment buildings of the time, the front and rear entrances to The Maitlands were never locked. The "No Soliciting" sign was a sufficient deterrent to undesirables. The idea of anyone being brazen enough to come into a residential building for the purpose of committing a criminal act was beyond the imagination of most people, including the rounders.

It's a thirty-five-minute walk to The Maitlands from the west end of Simpson Avenue in the working-class neighbourhood bisected by railroad tracks just north of Gerrard Street near Broadview Avenue. There, twenty-year-old Gerald Blair rented a small room in a three-storey brown brick house built just after the First World War.

On Sunday, October 17, Blair left home neatly dressed in a clean shirt, sports jacket, and slacks, and without any particular destination in mind at all. The young Brockville native with the brown wavy hair and wholesome Andy Hardy good looks was at loose ends in a town where the Lord's Day Act remained strictly in force. Only the odd corner store was permitted to remain open for business, and most entertainment venues were closed so as not to tempt the citizenry from their Sabbath duties. With nothing special to do and nowhere to go, he wandered aimlessly up and down the tree-lined streets near Yonge and Wellesley until he found himself standing under the portico of 36 Maitland.

He opened the front door and stepped inside. On his right was a bank of mailboxes, each of which bore the name and apartment number of a tenant. He ran his finger along the mailboxes until he found one that read "Olive Revell." Her name meant nothing to him, but the fact that she was a woman who in all likelihood lived alone did. If the name on the mailbox had read simply "Revell," perhaps his finger would not have paused there, and his random search would have yielded the name of someone else.

He made a mental note of her apartment number, then searched for the corresponding number on the floor above hers. He found it. The tenant on the upper floor was a man. He mentally recorded his name also, then began to search for Olive Revell's apartment.

Blair encountered no one as he walked the halls. But even if he had, it's doubtful that he'd have aroused suspicion. Gerald Blair looked like any other clean-cut kid who might have come to The Maitlands that Sunday afternoon to look in on an aunt or uncle, or an aging grandparent. In fact, he was nothing of the sort. Blair was already a veteran of Kingston Penitentiary, where he'd done time for battering and attempting to rape a twenty-four-year-old Brockville woman when he was just sixteen. He was a deeply troubled and dangerous young man who was often unable to control the violent forces that raged just beneath the surface.

Blair grew up in a tough section of Brockville, right across the street from the coal sheds that stood along the waterfront. They were his playground, his hideout. But the sheds were also forbidden territory for small boys who were supposed to be in school. The men who worked there couldn't keep him out. He was small for his age and became skilled at climbing and wiggling his tiny athletic body through small openings. No matter how many times he was turfed off the property, he always returned. Eventually, the owners of the coal sheds had had enough, and six-year-old Gerald Blair got a stern lecture from a Brockville police constable about skipping school, trespassing, and stealing. It would be the first of many encounters with the police throughout his childhood and adolescence, and many of these would lead to stints in what used to be called reform school, in Cobourg and Guelph. Young Gerald had no supervision at home. His parents could not control him. By the time he was eight years old, he took to running the streets until midnight, if he came home at all. Predictably, he graduated from trespassing to shoplifting, and from petty theft to breaking and entering, and finally to arson and auto theft.

After his release from Kingston for the assault and attempted rape, he stole a truck, and for a month he haunted the back roads and highways around Brockville, eluding capture until, in a spectacular crash that left the stolen truck a mangled wreck, he nearly killed himself and a passenger. As soon as he got out of hospital, he was tried and sent to jail for that offence. After serving his sentence, he went to Winnipeg, where he was arrested for housebreaking and sentenced to penitentiary in Manitoba. As he prowled the hallways of The Maitlands that Sunday afternoon, looking for Olive Revell's apartment, it had been five weeks since he'd gotten out of the pen.

He found her apartment and knocked on the door. When she opened it, he asked for the man whose name corresponded with the apartment directly above Olive's. Of course, she told Blair that the man he inquired after lived upstairs. As he thanked her and turned away, she smiled at him pleasantly and closed her door. He climbed the stairs to the next floor and walked the entire length of the hallway before retracing his steps to Olive's door.

He knocked again.

When Olive Revell didn't show up for work on Monday, her boss became concerned. This wasn't like her. She was never late, and had never taken time off. He drove to The Maitlands and found the building superintendent, who opened her apartment door just wide enough to permit him to peek inside and call her name.

No answer. The two men left.

When he returned to his law office, Olive's boss called the police to report her missing. But because details were so vague and the possibility existed that some weekend activity may have unexpectedly delayed her, it was agreed that no missing person report would be taken at that time.

The following day, however, when Olive failed once more to show up for work, the police were called again – this time, to her apartment. Constable Ron MacLachlan, who was patrolling in the area on his motorcycle, pulled up in front of The Maitlands and was met by the building superintendent, who guided him to the apartment and opened the door.

They found her lying face-up in the bathtub. She was dead.

Olive's body was clothed in a brassiere, blouse, panties, stockings, and slacks. MacLachlan could see there had been water in the bathtub, and though the plug was still in the drain, all the water had seeped away. He could also see that her clothes, once soaked, were now completely dry. Whatever had happened to her must have occurred two days before.

When detectives from 52 Division arrived to take over the investigation, they looked around the small one-bedroom apartment, and could see that it was neat and tidy, and that there did not appear to be any evidence that a struggle had taken place, although when they moved Olive's body, they noticed blood on the tub beneath her and in her hair. She had apparently bled from her right ear. Small amounts of blood were discovered on a white bedspread and green pillowcase that were found on the floor beside the bed.

While Ident officers searched in vain for fingerprints, her body was taken to the morgue, where a postmortem performed by Dr. Frederick Jaffe pointed to drowning as the cause of death. Dr. Jaffe told the investigators that bleeding from the ear is consistent with drowning.

The clothes that Olive wore when she died, the bloodstained bedspread and pillowcase, and numerous other exhibits were taken to the crime lab for analysis. The following day, blood specialist Elgin Brown went with detectives to the scene to search for any other blood-related clues that might shed light on the investigation. Nothing conclusive was found.

All of the victim's family, friends, and neighbours were interviewed, but nothing they said offered investigators a better explanation as to why or how this woman had died than the one suggested by the postmortem and their own observations.

What did they know?

After a careful search of the apartment, they found no evidence of a struggle; the apartment door had been locked and there was no sign of forced entry through the door or any of the windows; the bathtub had contained water, which had drained out due to a faulty plug; the slacks Olive wore had been immersed long enough in the water to dye her skin red, thus making a proper examination for bruises, abrasions, and sexual interference virtually impossible, though a very small bruise on her right temple was found; her neighbours in the building heard nothing from her apartment that would have led them to believe she was in trouble; there were no signs of significant injury to any part of her body, with the exception of the slight bruise on her temple and the bleeding from her right ear, which was already known to be consistent with drowning; she was fully clothed and did not appear to have been manhandled.

The detectives were left to theorize that Olive Revell had stumbled in the bedroom and struck her head. Analysis of the contents of her stomach revealed that she had taken headache medicine. Expert examination revealed that the blood on the pillowcase was mixed with saliva, and the investigators surmised that she may have tried to stem the flow of blood from a small, and later undetectable, cut inside her mouth, caused when she fell, by dabbing at it with the pillowcase. They then speculated that she wandered in a daze into the bathroom, where she had already drawn a bath, slipped on the bathmat, which was found askew, and fell unconscious into the water-filled tub and drowned.

But certain members of Olive's family weren't convinced her death was accidental. The investigators remained on the case, pursuing every lead, no matter how flimsy. In the end, however, they concluded that Olive Revell's death was, indeed, accidental. The case received no publicity. Olive's death notice was the only thing that appeared in the papers: "REVELL, Olive – Suddenly at her home . . ."

It was now November 1972. A tiny, distraught eighty-two-year-old woman lay whimpering pathetically and staring in abject terror at the ceiling of a hospital room in Brockville. She had been the victim of a savage sexual assault that had taken place in the senior citizens' residence where she lived. Her doctors weren't sure that she would survive the attack. Though she had been terribly shaken, the woman still managed to give police a description of the man who had assaulted her, and it wasn't long before she was able to identify him through photographs as Gerald Blair.

Blair was a patient at the psychiatric hospital in Brockville, where, one month before, doctors had decided to allow him out on weekend passes. It was during one of those passes that he raped and sodomized the elderly woman. Brockville police wasted no time in grabbing him off the street and throwing him in the cells.

This was the fifth time since that Sunday afternoon in 1965, when he knocked on Olive Revell's door, that Gerald Blair had been arrested for attacking, injuring, or raping a woman. Always his victims were vulnerable, unsuspecting strangers. Always his attacks on them were sudden and savage. Always he went for the throat first.

He appeared before a judge and was remanded to the hospital at Penetanguishene.

Six weeks after Blair's arrest, Detective Sergeant Curtiss and Corporal Berthiaume of the Brockville Police Force went to Penetang to interview him about the attack on the elderly woman who, by that time, had begun to make a slow recovery from her physical injuries, though one wonders if she would ever overcome the psychological trauma to which Blair had so brutally subjected her.

He gave them a written confession and signed it. But he had much more to say. He recited a lengthy list of criminal offences that he said he'd committed over the years, and which he wanted to get off his chest – among them the rape and murder of a woman named Olive seven years before in Toronto. He told them, somewhat smugly, that he'd made it look like an accidental drowning.

"I gave the bathmat a kick so it'd look like she slipped."

The following day, Jack McBride and I got a call from Curtiss. It didn't take long before we were able to match the information Curtiss gave us with the 1965 report on Olive Revell's death.

Gerald Blair's story was done. The departmental statement forms I'd brought to the hospital to record in longhand everything he had to say were now full. He had dictated to me slowly, without emotion, and with deliberately chosen words, how he repeatedly and methodically raped and finally strangled Olive Revell to death in The Maitlands seven years before.

Frequently, during the course of the fourteen-page confession, he would pause and say, "Just a min." Then, after thinking for a moment and forcing his memory to dredge up images, he would resume his story, taking great care to recall even the smallest details of Olive's apartment, which he diagrammed with amazing accuracy. He recalled the placement of furniture, the location of windows and doors, what was in the refrigerator and on the kitchen table, and a photograph that stood on her dresser of Olive and some friends in their 48th Highlander uniforms.

There was no doubt this man had been in Olive Revell's apartment on or about the date of the murder. He described it almost perfectly. But it was his description of Olive, what she wore, and how and where her body was found, that confirmed Gerald Blair as the murderer.

He told us that while he was sexually assaulting her, he had gagged her with the green pillowcase. After the initial assault, he walked her to the kitchen, where he gave her a glass of water and a couple of headache tablets. Both of these pieces of information confirmed the crime lab's findings that the pillowcase bore evidence of saliva and blood, and that the contents of Olive's stomach included traces of a headache medication.

Blair stole Olive's rent money from her purse and drank some of her liquor while he watched a few minutes of television. Then he forced her to return to the bedroom, where he punched her in the stomach and sexually assaulted her once more before strangling her, first with his hands, then with a nylon stocking. He had tightened the stocking around her neck aided by a small piece of wood, the significance of which had not been understood by police when it was found at the crime scene.

When she was dead, Blair straightened her clothing, then went into the bathroom and turned on the water. He waited until the tub was almost full, then carried her body into the bathroom, immersed it in the water, turned off the taps and kicked the bathmat askew. He returned to the living room where he relaxed for some time, smoking a few more cigarettes and watching television. Then he went from room to room systematically destroying every trace of his presence in the apartment. He wiped everything he had touched, not once but twice, before turning out all the lights and leaving, making sure to lock the door behind him.

It was growing dark by the time Blair finished his statement, so Jack got up to turn on the lights. After nearly three hours in the tiny closet of a room, there was barely a lungful of breathable air left. Tobacco smoke hung in thick motionless clouds. The small window that had given inmates in the corridor a ringside seat to our interview had become fogged over with condensation from their breath. Outside, the howling wind blew snow horizontally across the now completely buried hospital grounds.

I don't mind admitting that by that time, both Jack and I wanted nothing more than to escape that claustrophobic little chamber, the demented watchers at the window, and the off-the-wall, needle-toting pirate who presided over them. The place was enough to give anyone the willies. We agreed that we'd gladly take our chances with the snowstorm rather than spend even one more minute at Penetang.

Blair read and signed his statement, then asked to speak to the doctor, who had returned and was just outside the door. As Jack and I left the room, the watchers sullenly turned away from the window and went back to prowling the corridor.

More than a year later, at the Supreme Court building on Queen Street, a hearing was held to determine Gerald Blair's mental fitness to stand trial on the Revell murder charge. After three days of testimony from police officers and psychiatrists, who said Blair had made numerous unsubstantiated claims that he was a mass murderer responsible for the deaths of more than twenty-one people, he took the stand himself, claiming, "I'm not quite as senseless as other people would like to fool each other into believing I am. I haven't killed anyone!"

The jury deliberated for only an hour before declaring him not guilty by reason of insanity.

Three psychiatrists who testified at the hearing agreed that Gerald Blair suffered from acute and chronic mental disorders so profound as to render any notion of a cure unrealistic.

He was sent back to Penetang, protesting his innocence all the way.

6

"5–2–1"

I *have never put any store in the alleged role of the occult in human* *affairs. And though experience has persuaded me — just as it has most* *other police officers, emergency room nurses, and cab drivers — that a full moon* *brings out the lunatics, I have always discounted completely the notion that the* *supernatural has ever been a factor in any homicide investigation of mine.*

Having made that bold assertion, I can neither deny nor explain the strange *coincidence that seemed to pursue Jack McBride and me when, one weekend in* *the spring of 1976, we were obliged to investigate the sudden and tragic deaths* *of no fewer than six people around the city — six people who shared a curious* *numerological link.*

It was four-thirty on a Saturday morning when my bedside telephone rang.

The stentorian voice blaring over the line belonged to Sergeant of Detectives John Standing, a man who had no need of a phone to summon me downtown from my east end home. He had merely to stand out on Church Street and bellow for all of Scarborough to hear him.

"BILL, IT'S JOHN STANDING."

"Morning, Sarge."

"WERE YOU ASLEEP, BILL?"

"As a matter of fact, Sarge, I was. Just dozing, though," I lied, as though sleeping soundly were near the bottom of the list of things I'd rather do at that time of the bloody morning!

"WELL, BILL, YOU'D BETTER GET OUT OF BED NOW AND COME DOWN TO HEADQUARTERS. WE HAVE A LITTLE JOB FOR YOU TO DO. I'LL FILL YOU IN WHEN YOU GET HERE."

"Okay, Sarge," I yawned. "I'll just give Jack McBride a call. We're working together this weekend."

"NO NEED, BILL. I ALREADY CALLED JACK'S HOUSE. IT SOUNDED TO ME LIKE HE WAS ASLEEP, TOO."

"No kidding."

"WHAT WAS THAT, BILL?"

"Nothing, Sarge. I'll pick Jack up on the way in."

"THAT'LL BE JUST FINE, BILL, JUST FINE!"

Fifteen minutes later, still munching on a hastily buttered piece of toast, I pulled up in front of Jack's darkened house in my little Nash Rambler – a car he had grown to hate because there wasn't enough room for both of us to sit shoulder to shoulder, facing forward. Instead, and with a great deal of complaining, he had to hunker over to the right, with his entire weight resting on one buttock, which I always reckoned was a small enough price to pay for the money-saving privilege of leaving his car at home.

That morning, Jack banged his head, as he so often did, struggling to get comfortable.

"*Shit, Bill!* When are you gonna get a decent set of wheels?"

"A third-class ride's better than a first-class walk, any day," I chirped.

"Don't you ever get embarrassed?"

"You ex-Traffic men are all the same: you've got entirely too much respect for automobiles. You're in love with the damned things, for heaven's sake! Anyway, who's gonna see us at this time of day?"

"Your trouble is you have no shame."

"No, my trouble is I have no money."

He lit a cigarette and glowered out the window in silence until we got to Headquarters.

Such is life in Homicide, where there are few perks. However, when I was on the squad, there was one: when we had to work weekends, we could pick our own hours. We could come in at any time, as long as we put in the requisite minimum eight hours. Jack and I had planned to start work that morning at ten o'clock, and stay until six that evening hammering out the crown brief on an upcoming court case. Instead, after a quick briefing from John Standing, we found ourselves at five-thirty tiptoeing down the hall of one of the larger hotels in the city, trying not to disturb the sleep of guests who were innocent of the fact that only a few paces from where they lay in blissful slumber, the bodies of an elderly man and woman had been discovered by the night manager, who had been drawn by the foul smell emanating from suite 521.

The sickly sweet stench of death was palpable as we entered the room. The body of the woman was in the bed, while that of her husband sat in a chair, fully clothed. We guessed that the old dears had been dead about three days, and their blackened bodies, which had bloated to twice normal size, bore no similarities to the silver-haired couple in their mid-eighties who smiled warmly from a gilt-framed photograph on the dresser. In the bottom drawer of that same dresser, we found a half-carton of milk, now soured, a shriveled head of lettuce, and a mouldy loaf of bread. All of these sat in a couple of inches of rancid water. The drawer had been lined with a green garbage bag, and had apparently served as a makeshift refrigerator. Though we found ample evidence to indicate that the couple had been wealthy, they had chosen to live a frugal, even ascetic, existence as residents of the aging hostelry.

They'd left a note saying that the unremitting pain and loss of dignity through which the poor woman had suffered for the better part of a year had become too much for her to bear. Her husband, who had assumed the responsibility for her care, was failing himself. Life was becoming too heavy a burden for both of them. She had asked him to help her end the misery. For nearly seventy years they had loved one another. Life without her was unthinkable. He would go with her. He'd given her an overdose of sleeping pills, then swallowed the rest himself. Together they had lived, and together they had slipped mercifully away on their own terms.

Notwithstanding the arguably poetic nature of their act and the moving letter that explained it, the law and our own professionalism compelled Jack and me to separate any personal feelings we might have had about the matter, and to treat what had happened as a murder-suicide. Though there would be no arrest or trial, we could not close the book on this case until we had investigated the matter thoroughly, beginning with a closer look at the bodies to assure ourselves that the facts supported what we'd read in the letter.

Jack had not worked Homicide for very long. Even though he outranked me, he was junior to me on the squad. I had been assigned by our commander, George Sellar, to train him. And though, as a seasoned traffic accident investigator and detective, he was accustomed to dealing with dead bodies, handling those in an advanced stage of decomposition was something else again!

I made much of removing a pen from the breast pocket of my suit jacket, and standing with it poised above my notebook, as if ready to write. Of course, the inference was immediately clear to Jack: it must be *he* who handled the bodies, cautiously easing them from side to side, and up and down, in search of any outward signs of violence.

"I don't mind taking the notes this time," he offered hopefully.

"Nice try," I sneered.

"Sonofa . . ."

Dolefully, he pulled on the heavy rubber gloves we carried in our kit for occasions such as this, and sidled up beside the seated corpse. I watched him while he futzed around for a minute or two, then decided to prod him a bit.

"Just like a traffic man, always looking for a driver's licence."

"Bugger off, will you! This is disgusting!"

He didn't need to tell me. I'd moved my share of bloated corpses, and understood all too well that great care must be taken not to jostle them. Otherwise, they could explode, and you could end up with a faceful of noxious, foul-smelling gases – and much worse!

At last, and with much grunting and clenched-teeth cursing, Jack completed his examination of both bodies. By then, the Ident boys had come and were busying themselves around the place. I was grateful that they'd talked the hotel management into providing us with some coffee, but Jack, who usually enjoyed a cup as much as the next guy, didn't seem to want any for some reason.

A little before ten, we had the corpses removed to the morgue. By noon, we were back at Headquarters. No sooner had we begun banging out our report about the incident to Chief Harold Adamson, than the phone rang.

Jack picked up the receiver.

"Homicide, Detective Sergeant McBride."

As he listened, Jack scribbled notes on a scrap piece of paper, then to the caller he said, "There's just McCormack and me, we're it. (Pause) Okay, we'll head right out."

Five minutes later, we were dodging the weekend traffic on Danforth Avenue before turning up a major north–south street in search of a house in which a woman's body had been seen sprawled across the kitchen floor by a neighbour peering through the front door. It was twelve-thirty when Jack and I pulled up in front of number 521.

The kitchen was a chamber of horrors. Lying face-down in the middle of a floor awash with blood and water that had overflowed the sink was the body of a pretty blonde woman in her early thirties. A knife was buried in her chest beneath the left armpit. She had been dead an hour or two.

Within minutes of our arrival, we were joined at the scene by Dr. John Bunt, as able a coroner as ever I've worked with, and one who had a flair for investigation. He leaned over the woman, who was obviously dead, and performed the necessary examinations to make an official pronouncement. Then he stepped back into the front hall beside Jack and me, taking great care not to disturb any evidence. For several minutes, all of us surveyed every inch of the blood-spattered kitchen. The ceiling, the cupboard doors, the countertop and table, and of course the floor, had literally been sprayed with blood as if shot from a hose. There was not a single surface in the entire room that did not have blood on it.

The first officer on the scene, a young uniformed man from 56 Division, told us that when he had entered the kitchen and found the woman, the cold water tap was running full force, and because a dishrag and a partially cut up chicken in the sink had blocked the drain, water had cascaded over the rim and had run over most of the floor. He had reached across the body and turned off the tap before bending to the woman to discover the knife buried up to the hilt in her chest. He'd felt in vain for a pulse, and could see by her waxen skin that she had bled almost white, so he ran to his cruiser and radioed for his sergeant, the coroner, and, just in case there was still some life in her, an ambulance.

From our vantage point in the front hall, we could see a part bottle of whiskey on the kitchen counter; beside the bottle was a highball glass that appeared to have whiskey in it. The rim of the glass bore traces of the same shade of pink lipstick that was on the body's lips. Apparently, the woman had been drinking while cutting up the chicken, which, to the best of our reckoning, must have been before ten that morning, maybe even earlier.

Judging from the condition in which we found the rest of the neat little bungalow, the woman and her husband – who was nowhere in sight – kept a meticulously clean and orderly household. We could see, despite the presence of so much blood, that the kitchen had been scrubbed spotless prior to whatever had occurred there. Those few square feet of tile floor that weren't sluiced with blood and water bore only the shoe prints of the victim and the size eleven boot prints of the young uniformed man, who retraced for us every step he had taken while he was in the room. Since he had not permitted anyone else to enter until Dr. Bunt's arrival, we were certain that no one else had been in that kitchen.

Slowly, the bizarre answer to the mystery of this woman's violent death began to reveal itself. With the help of her genuinely distraught husband, who, on returning home, proved to us that he'd been golfing with a group of friends, we were able to reconstruct what had happened.

The victim was known to drink alone, sometimes too early in the day, and too much. It was about eight that morning when her husband kissed her good-bye and headed out the door to the golf course. She was about to cut up a chicken, which she intended to marinate for a late afternoon barbecue.

It seems she'd taken a drink or two and had begun carving up the bird under the cold water tap when she cut her left index finger badly with the knife, nearly slicing off the end of it. Blood had been smeared on and around the handle of one cupboard door above the counter. Inside this cupboard we found a box of Band-Aids. Clearly, she had intended to patch herself up. But then things went from bad to worse – and very quickly!

Her left wrist above the thumb bore a deep gash, which had severed a major blood vessel. The ceiling directly above the cupboard door had been sprayed with blood, as had the walls and the floor close by, indicating that the woman had inadvertently slashed herself on the wrist while she was reaching for the Band-Aids. It then appeared, from tracks made in the blood on the floor, that she had wheeled about and had begun to scramble from the kitchen in search of help. But she'd slipped on her own blood and fallen upon the knife, burying it deep in her chest, bringing about her own senseless and completely accidental death.

Since Jack and I and the coroner were all satisfied that this was not a homicide, we called in the divisional detectives to finish the investigation. It was now about five in the afternoon, and we'd been on duty for twelve hours. We decided to head for home, intending to come in early Sunday morning for the autopsies on the elderly couple found in the hotel.

We left my little Nash Rambler in the police parking lot, having been given the rare privilege of taking the police car home by the magnanimous, if somewhat noisy, John Standing.

"SURE, BOYS, TAKE THE CRUISER HOME. THAT WAY, YOU CAN GET HERE ON THE DOUBLE, IF I NEED YOU."

We were inches from home, each of us yearning for a hot shower and a decent meal, when the dispatcher nailed us:

"D-two, call."

Jack reached for the mike.

"Waddyah doin'?!" I snarled, knowing full well we had no choice but to answer the dispatcher.

"What's it look like I'm doin'? We got a call, for Pete's sake!" Then, into the mike, "D-two, go ahead."

"Go to a phone and call Sergeant of Detectives Standing."

"D-two, ten-four."

Knowing the news media all listened in on police calls, the radio room never transmitted sensitive information to Homicide Squad officers on the air, which would have drawn reporters to us like flies to a road apple. I found a phone booth on St. Clair Avenue and pulled the cruiser over to the curb, where Jack got out. He slipped a coin into the slot and wearily dialed the number. Minutes later, he returned to the cruiser and slumped into the passenger seat, shaking his head.

"Well?"

"Guy just shot his wife and little girl to death. The ten-year-old son got away when the neighbours barged in and grabbed him. Detectives from 41 Division have him at the station. I said we'd head to the apartment first."

"Sweet mother of Jesus! The wife *and* little girl?"

Jack nodded sadly. There was nothing worse than investigating the murder of a child — nothing! He gave me the street address of the large publicly subsidized apartment complex in which the shootings had occurred, but not the apartment number, so when we walked through the lobby of the building, past two uniformed men who'd been posted there, I asked him which unit we wanted.

"You won't believe me when I tell you."

"Not 521, surely."

"Apartment 521."

As we rode the elevator up to the fifth floor, I couldn't shake the feeling that Jack and I were being mocked by perverse and unseen forces that compelled us to dog the trail of a series of tragic coincidences. It was as though the five people who had died had been doomed simply because they shared the same numerals in their addresses.

Shocked, anguished faces stared from the doors of every apartment we walked past on the floor where the shootings had taken place. The little girl and her mother had had many friends in the building, and already they were being mourned. The wife of one of the men who had rushed heroically into the apartment and wrestled the gun from the man's hands, thereby preventing him from shooting his son as well, sat on the couch in her living room cradling the little boy in her arms. She rocked him gently back and forth, trying to calm his breathing, which came in deep, convulsive gasps.

It was indeed a grim scene that greeted us in the apartment. The man had chased his wife from room to room and had shot her as she was about to run out the door. She had taken the full charge of a shotgun blast in the back. He then pursued his children, cornering his six-year-old daughter in the bathroom, where the little mite had cowered in terror beneath the sink. She died instantly, still clutching her dolly. Before he could shoot the boy, a half-dozen of his neighbours had swarmed into the apartment and tackled the muscular six-footer, snatching the gun away. He put up a ferocious fight until uniformed officers from 41 Division arrived. One of them had to stun him with a fist to the jaw before he could be subdued and handcuffed.

It was eleven that night when Jack and I walked through the front door of 41 Division and stood in front of the desk sergeant.

"Where is he?" I asked, far too weary for the usual pleasantries.

"In the bucket. I put a PC outside the cell in case he tried to do himself in."

"Has anybody else been near him since he was locked up?"

"Just my station duty operator. He took the guy a coffee about an hour ago. We made a note of it."

"What kind of shape's he in?"

"If you mean mental, he's off his bloody rocker, if you ask me!"

And so he was. When we took the man out of the cells and walked him to the small interview room off the main detective office, it quickly became clear to Jack and me that we were dealing with someone who had absolutely no appreciation of what he had done. His wife and little girl were nothing more than possessions, chattels to do with what he would. He was furious with his neighbours for invading his privacy, and with the police for placing him under arrest.

"That was my place, *my* place!" he yelled, angrily stabbing his chest with a finger. "I pay the rent there. Those bastards had no right to come into my home, or to bring me here. What I do in my own place is none of their damned business. *None!*"

He was surely one of the most belligerent and remorseless human beings I ever had the misfortune to deal with. But, as George Sellar had so often reminded everyone under his command, good investigators keep their personal feelings to themselves. We had a job to do, and we were determined to do it right. Regardless of this man's state of mind or his provoking behaviour, he must be given an opportunity to respond to the charges before him.

I cautioned him on two counts of murder, then asked if he understood the charges, and if he had anything to say. His response was a rambling, disjointed harangue against life in general and his wife in particular. He told us he used to work up north in the bush as a lumberjack, but his fortunes had taken a nose-dive when he injured himself and was forced to seek employment in the city, where he felt like a caged bear. He raged on in this fashion, ignoring completely any questions I put to him about the shootings.

Jack and I soon realized we weren't going to get a statement from the man, and were about to return him to the cells, when he said something that floored both of us.

"You guys can do what the hell you want because I killed the sonofabitch who caused all this, anyway."

"You did what?" Jack asked, his eyes wide with shock.

"I killed the sonofabitch, I told you! Went to his place and shot him right through the heart."

"When?"

"This morning."

"Who did you kill?" I asked.

"The fuckin' postman. Who do you think? He was bangin' the wife. Neither of them thought I knew, but I did. So I followed him home last week and found out where he lived. Then this morning I drove out there nice and early and shot him. *Pop!*"

Defiantly, he gave us an address of a rooming house in the city's west end. Jack arranged to have a couple of uniformed men from 12 Division go to the house. No one answered their knock, so the officers entered by a side door. When they encountered no one on the main floor, they climbed the stairs and began a room-to-room search of the second floor. In the third room, they found the body of a man lying on the bed. He had died from a single gunshot wound in the middle of his chest. His face was a mask of wide-eyed disbelief.

There was no point in questioning our suspect further that night, so we lodged him in the cells and dragged our weary bones to the rooming house. We got there at about two in the morning. Our arrival was preceded by that of a brand new coroner who, out of respect for the dead man, had chastely covered his body up with a woollen blanket after making a pronouncement of death.

I entered the bedroom, and let out a bellow that threatened to awaken the poor fellow.

"WHO THE HELL PUT THAT DAMNED BLANKET ON THE BODY?"

From behind me came the rather timid voice of the rookie coroner – a compassionate and highly respected family physician with whom I was destined to become fast friends in the years that followed.

"I'm afraid I did."

"WELL, IN DOING SO, DOCTOR, YOU HAVE CONTAMINATED *MY* BODY!"

The coroner was mortified.

"Oh! I'm awfully sorry, Detective McCormack. I had no idea."

It was six-thirty Sunday morning before Jack McBride and I got back to Headquarters and began hammering out our reports to the chief on the events of the last twenty-six hours. At about nine o'clock, we got a call from Dr. Hudson, the pathologist who was scheduled to perform the autopsies on the elderly couple found in the hotel, and on the woman who had accidentally stabbed herself to death. When we told him about the other three bodies, we agreed that all six autopsies would be conducted on Monday.

At ten, we slapped our reports down on the inspector's desk and headed for home, with Jack whining all the way about the perils of riding in my little Nash Rambler. Sunday was a lost day for both of us.

When we reported for work on Monday morning at eight o'clock, we had six postmortems to look forward to.

Just as Jack and I were preparing to leave the office Monday afternoon, one of the other detectives handed me a phone message. It was from the only living relative – and a distant one at that – of the elderly woman in the hotel. She had called from New York City to say she and her husband were flying in this morning, and wished to talk to Jack and me about any "property" we might have found in the hotel suite.

"What's she after?" I asked.

"Apparently the woman had a diamond ring that was pretty spectacular. The big city cousin thinks she should take care of it."

If she could prove she was the next of kin, the ring would go to her. When we told the pathologist, he looked dubiously at the swollen fingers of the deceased. But after performing a rather quick procedure, he dropped a ring with a rock the size of a walnut into a glass jar and said, "This what you're looking for?"

Later that afternoon, with all the autopsies completed, Jack and I were back at Headquarters. Sitting outside the Homicide office was a well-dressed couple in their mid-seventies. The man rolled a fat cigar around in his mouth, while the woman dabbed at dry eyes with a linen handkerchief.

We introduced ourselves and invited the couple to have a seat in one of the interview rooms, where Jack produced the small glass jar containing the diamond ring. He removed the lid, filling the room and the adjacent office with the same foul odour that had greeted us on our arrival at the hotel suite two days before. It was enough to make a strong man swoon.

But not the grieving cousin. Calmly, she fished the ring out of the jar and, without so much as a perfunctory wipe with her handkerchief, slid it on her finger. And then, as if to assure us, she volunteered, "I know she would have wanted me to have it."

7

The Hooker Murder

In the neighbourhood of Jarvis and Dundas Streets there used to stand a half-dozen or so fleabag hotels that catered to the sex trade. They were tough, unfriendly places that attracted a low-calibre clientele, where brawls were routine and everybody was on the make, especially the hookers. Hustling tricks in places where most of the patrons were known criminals and the police entered only in pairs was a dangerous way for the women to make a living. They put their lives on the line every night because they never really knew what their next john had in mind.

It was a cold night in April 1977. Bonnie's john had gotten everything he'd come for and was pulling on his pants when the screaming started in the room next door.

"Please, no! Oh, my God! No!"

Bonnie reached across the sagging bed and lifted the telephone receiver. She was automatically connected to the front desk, where a twenty-three-year-old clerk sat thumbing through a skin magazine.

"Yeah, what?"

"You mean you can't hear anything? The girl in room 225 sounds like she's getting killed or something. You better check it out."

"Oh, for cryin' out —"

"Do it now, dip-shit, she's screamin'!"

As the desk clerk hung up on Bonnie, the switchboard buzzed and the light for room 225 blinked. The clerk answered it.

"What's goin' on in there?"

But all he could hear was the receiver at the other end bouncing off something hard — maybe the night table, maybe the floor — and a woman's voice pleading, "No! Please don't!"

Bonnie's john was a nickel-and-dime lawyer who defended nothing but punks and hookers in the Old City Hall courts. He'd pleaded her guilty a couple of days earlier to boosting a box of hair colouring from Eaton's. Since it was her first shoplifting offence, she'd received a fine instead of time. But he'd managed to convince her she had him to thank, so tonight's interlude in the grungy room at Larry's Hideaway was a freebie.

He yanked an inside-out turtleneck over his head, jammed his feet into a pair of loafers and, as he rushed to the door, snatched up the duffel coat that hung over a chair.

"I'm gone. See you around."

"You chicken-shit bastard! Aren't you even going to help her?"

"Are you crazy?"

He scuttled out the door and down the hall.

Though the room occupied by the screaming hooker was just thirty paces from the front desk, straight down the hall, the young desk clerk dared not enter it himself. Instead, he phoned the bar downstairs and asked Jack, the night manager, and one of the bouncers for help.

"Come on up here, we got trouble."

As a form of cheap insurance, the smart girls usually tipped hotel bouncers, barmen, and front desk staff a few bucks every now and then. That way, if one of their johns turned ugly, they had an outside chance of getting help – assuming they were able to call for it. In reality, the fleabag hotels on or near Jarvis Street that used to let "working girls" service their "dates" in grungy rooms rented by the half-hour offered scant protection.

The nature of their work compels hookers to be alone with, and completely at the mercy of, strangers whose sexual "tastes" can, at times, be nothing short of depraved. Prostitutes routinely get their teeth knocked out, their eyes blackened, or their faces slashed by their customers. And while pimps pretend to offer their girls some measure of protection, the fact is that they are nothing but leeches who pose more of a risk of violence than most johns. Generally, though, squabbles between hookers and johns seldom amount to much. And sometimes, as with an incident that took place in the Ford Hotel – which stood, when I was a young beatman, across from the bus terminal at Bay and Dundas Streets – the confrontations could even be comical.

At the Ford, one of the girls was having trouble with a drunken john who thought he was paying too much for what she was delivering. Together they set up a ruckus that could be heard from one end of the hall to the other. Before long, two beefy "doormen" barged into the room. Like bouncers everywhere, these two *liked* trouble – first, because it was their bread and butter, and second, because they harboured the erroneous belief that the law allowed them to beat the snot out of people and get away with it.

As soon as he saw these two bruisers come through the door, the john went squirrelly and started jumping around the room, knocking over furniture and throwing things. After chasing him around for a few minutes, they finally cornered him in the clothes closet, where they proceeded to slap him silly before dragging him into an elevator and tossing him ass-first into the alley.

"You come back here, you whistleprick, you're gonna need an ambulance!"

"Screw you!" he shot back, then picked himself up and limped, rumpled and shoeless, towards the sidewalk. I happened to be in the alley at the time. I was standing under a lamppost, writing in my notebook, when he caught sight of me.

"Fly's undone," I offered.

"And screw you, too!" he yelled, still fighting mad.

He was clearly determined to get himself into more trouble that night, so to save him the grief, I pinched him as a common drunk and marched him back to the station to nurse his bruises and sleep it off in the bullpen.

I never saw the hooker he'd been arguing with, but a cabby told me a couple of days later that she was furious with the bouncers for taking too long to come to her aid. As they were muscling the yahoo out of the room, she sat unabashed on the toilet with the bathroom door wide open and screeched at them like a harpy. On her way out of the hotel, she gave them both the finger, then took a cab to the Warwick Hotel to hustle another trick.

That's how things were and always had been for the girls who worked these hard streets and crummy dives. But while there was no denying that hooking could be hazardous, as a rule, the girls were seldom seriously hurt or killed. The girl in room 225 of Larry's Hideaway would be the exception to that rule.

As Jack the night manager and the bouncer passed the front desk on their way to the room, the clerk grabbed the master key and handed it over. When they got to the room, Jack knocked hard on the door, then took a couple of steps back, just in case.

The door opened, and there stood a stocky, balding, middle-aged man wearing black horn-rimmed glasses. He was stripped to the waist and his hairy belly drooped heavily over the belt loops of a pair of faded green work pants. He held out two scarlet hands that appeared as though they'd been rinsed in blood up to the wrists and said, "I did it. I'm guilty."

Jack put his hand on the man's sweaty chest and pushed him aside. "Stand over there."

The man took three paces backward and stood stock still.

As Jack and the bouncers entered the room, a naked woman in her late twenties rose unsteadily from the bed and lurched towards them, both hands outstretched. Her entire body glistened with dark red blood, which ran freely from deep wounds on her chest and arms. She approached to within one foot of Jack, close enough for him to feel her laboured breath on his face. She opened her mouth to speak, but was able only to form the words, "Please help me."

The sight of her appalled him, and he could not bring himself to touch her.

"Sit down, sugar. You better sit down and relax."

Like a sleepy child who has stayed up far too late, she nodded and turned obediently towards the bed. It was then that Jack and the others saw the bone-handled knife buried to the hilt between her shoulder blades.

Jack turned to the desk clerk: "Get back to the switchboard and call an ambulance!"

"What about that phone?" asked the clerk, indicating the one in the room, whose receiver the girl had knocked off its cradle, and which she was now feebly trying to retrieve.

"I don't know. I don't think we should use it, 'cause the cops . . ."

Suddenly, the obvious struck the manager, and he turned again to the clerk, "You better call the cops, too."

The shocked boy forced himself to tear his eyes from the girl and raced down the hall.

Meanwhile, the bare-chested man made as though he were going to walk out of the room. One of the bouncers put an arm across the door to block his exit.

"Where do you think you're goin', asshole?"

With elaborate contempt, the man looked the bouncer up and down. But his bluff fooled no one – not even himself. He knew that if he dared to push things an inch further, he'd ignite the younger man's fuse. He forced a smile, shrugged his shoulders, and leaned against a wall as casually as if he were waiting for a bus.

But even that was almost too much for the bouncer to bear, and he took a step forward.

The manager caught hold of his arm. "You stay put! Just keep an eye on him until the cops get here."

The girl was sitting slouched over on the bed watching blood from a deep slash on her arm make a puddle on the dirty grey rug. She put the phone receiver up to her ear as though she were about to speak into it. But no words came out. She sighed and yawned deeply, then slowly collapsed backward, burying the knife further in her back.

"*Geez, no!*" Jack remained rooted to the spot, unable to bring himself to go to her.

The bare-chested man watched the girl impassively, then walked to the sill of the only window in the room, which was open about ten inches. He picked up a dirty blue ski jacket and leaned forward so that he could peer outside, then cast a tentative glance over his shoulder, seemingly weighing his chances of hoisting himself through the window to freedom. Not liking the odds, he turned once more in the direction of the door as if to leave. But the bouncer continued to block his path.

"Put those things down. You're not going anywhere."

Two blocks away, Constables Alison Buchanan and Stephen Craig were cruising past Maple Leaf Gardens towards Yonge Street. In another hour and a half, they'd be pulling their scout car into the 52 Division parking lot and booking off duty.

But the dispatcher had other plans: "Fifty-two-o-nine, call."

Buchanan: "Fifty-two-o-nine, go ahead."

Dispatcher: "Fifty-two-o-nine, a disturbance at Larry's Hideaway, 121 Carlton Street."

Buchanan: "Ten-four, dispatch."

Steve Craig did a slow U-turn in front of the Gardens and headed for the hotel. No sooner had he straightened the wheel than the dispatcher called again.

"We now have that as a stabbing, fifty-two-o-nine. Use caution. Ambulance on the way at 10:28 p.m."

Buchanan: "*Ten-four!*"

Craig jammed his foot down on the accelerator.

Dispatcher: "Other units in the area of Jarvis and Carlton, call. (Pause) Fifty-two-o-eight, where are you?" No response. "Fifty-one-o-three . . . you in the area?"

Scout car 5103 was manned by Constables John Billis and Larry McCoy. They were just a few blocks east, near Parliament Street.

"Fifty-one-o-three, go ahead."

Dispatcher: "Back up fifty-two-o-nine. Report of a stabbing, Larry's Hideaway."

"Ten-four."

Thirty seconds later, both scout cars pulled up to the curb in front of Larry's Hideaway and the officers walked briskly through the front door, their revolvers unholstered. They knew they would be joined in a few minutes by others from 51 and 52 Divisions.

In the lobby an excited young man waved his arms and shouted, "Over here! It's a bad one. The guy's still in there with her – room 225."

To the obvious consternation of the clerk, the officers slowed their pace. This was not safe territory; they could not let their guard down. In the hall outside room 225 Craig encountered the manager. After exchanging a few words, he and Buchanan entered the room.

Immediately inside the door was the bouncer. Still leaning against the wall was the bare-chested man. Lying motionless on her back was the naked girl. She was breathing shallowly.

Buchanan: "Where's the weapon?"

"It's in her back. The knife's still in her back," the bare-chested man replied in a voice devoid of emotion.

Steve Craig pushed him up against the wall and, after handcuffing him, walked him out of the room, across the hall, and into another room. After cautioning him, he kept conversation with the man to an absolute minimum. By that time, the ambulance had arrived and the attendants had lifted the wounded girl onto the stretcher. Though Wellesley Hospital was only one long city block away, it was no use, she'd lost too much blood. She was dead on arrival.

Herm Lowe and I got the call minutes later. We sent Bill Urie, another Homicide Squad member, to Wellesley Emergency to take charge of the body and interview everybody involved there. We headed to the hotel.

When we got there, we went to the room where Buchanan and Craig were holding the man they'd arrested. I told them to take him to the 51 Division detective office and to stay with him until we arrived. Moreover, they were to make certain no one else had direct contact with the man – no one, not even other police officers.

This was a precaution we always insisted on. Not only is it important to protect homicide suspects in police custody from acts of revenge committed by friends or relatives of their alleged victims, it is essential that every word an accused person says in relation to the offence be accurately recorded and introduced into evidence at trial. By failing to isolate an arrested suspect – at least until he has been thoroughly interviewed and given an opportunity to admit or deny the charge – investigators cannot testify with any certainty that the accused person wasn't induced, either by threat or promise, to confess. Of course, if the confession is compromised the court cannot, and should not, convict.

This precaution is taken very seriously by experienced police officers. I have many times seen uniformed staff sergeants march the route that would shortly be taken through a police station by an accused and his or her accompanying officers, and roust everybody out of sight – including the inspector! Rumour has it that in the course of one murder investigation years ago, such a pre-emptive sweep led to a rather testy exchange between a veteran staff sergeant and his younger superior – a man he'd trained years before. The inspector took offence to being hustled out of the way in his own station:

"Who the hell do you think you're talking to, you old fart? *I* run this place!"

"Well, you better not be standing there when they bring this guy through the back door."

"And what if I am?"

"First, I'll take a round outa yuh – and you know I still can – and then I'll make sure you get a witness subpoena so you can explain to the judge why you're bein' such a dickhead. Now, piss off!"

We watched as Buchanan and Craig walked the man down the hall to their cruiser, then we entered room 225 and directed the work of Ident officers as they fingerprinted, photographed, and measured everything of interest in the shabby little chamber.

On the windowsill, beneath a dazzling silver lamé coat, we found a purse containing identification in the name of Tracy LaSalle (not her real name), age twenty-eight. We gathered up these and other articles of clothing that had belonged to her – provocative lingerie and form-fitting slacks and a sweater that had highlighted the contours of her tall, slender figure. In life, these had been among the tools of her trade. Now that she was dead, they were just exhibits to be bagged and labelled.

Much of the girl's clothing had been doused with blood, which had gushed several feet from the four deep wounds on her body. Later that evening, Herm and I would take all the clothing and, of course, the bedclothes and hang them up to dry in the basement of Headquarters where we shared "locker" space with all the other Homicide teams. Each team was assigned a steel cage about the size of an average bed-room in which all manner of blood- and urine-soaked articles would be dried before depositing them at the lab. They had to be completely dry before the lab would take them. Consequently, some of these grim exhibits hung on clotheslines or sat in bins for several hours, even days, before they could be removed. If, as was often the case, we had had a particularly busy week, we'd find ourselves gingerly picking our way among the clotheslines with our faces mere inches away from sodden blankets, shirts, or jackets. Of course, the vile stench given off by the articles in those lockers would turn anyone's stomach.

All that awaited us, but for the next hour or two we interviewed the hotel employees, who told us everything that happened from the time the man walked into the hotel earlier that evening and registered under the name of Wilson to when the police arrived.

The bouncer couldn't get over how matter-of-fact the man had been. "I've never seen anything like it before. The guy was really calm. It was weird. He was just standing there. In fact, he even asked me for a cigarette." He shook his head in disbelief, then added, "I wanted to do something for the broad, but I thought I'd do more damage than good."

He was probably right. In any case, by the time he and the others got to her, it was already too late.

We let the hotel staff go about their business and sealed the room so that it could be examined in even greater detail later, then turned our attention to Tracy LaSalle's girlfriends, other hookers who worked this part of town. Bonnie was first. She'd been caught by a uniformed man while trying to sneak out through the back of Larry's Hideaway. She wasn't happy and took it out on Herm.

"I got no time for this shit!"

"You were turning a trick when you heard the screaming, is that right?"

"Just finished."

"The john, he heard it too?"

"Sure he heard it! I'll bet the whole friggin' hotel heard it."

"What's his name?"

"Are you kidding me?"

"Okay, so his name slips your mind, but I still need you to give us a statement."

"For Pete's sake, I'm late already!"

"It won't take long."

"Can I get a ride back to the Warwick when I'm done?"

"The Warwick? Sure."

Bonnie told us what she knew, which wasn't much, so Herm held up his end of the bargain and had a couple of uniformed officers drop her off outside the Warwick. They were going right past there anyway.

Though Bonnie didn't know Tracy well, the three other girls we talked to that night did, and every one of them said she was "something special." Even though they competed with her for tricks in low-rent places like the Westover, the Walsingham, and the Warwick, they all liked her. When they heard we were investigating her stabbing, they piled into a car and drove to Wellesley Hospital to do they knew not what. They just wanted to be there.

Bill Urie was already at the hospital, and had been present when the coroner pronounced Tracy dead. When the three girls showed up, he pulled out his notebook and started writing. He spoke first to Helen, a statuesque redhead, who turned over every dollar she made to the rotten little puke she lived with so he wouldn't smack her around.

"I noticed her as soon as she started working out of the Westover. She was outstanding! Tall and slim, and she had terrific hair. Sometimes it was platinum blonde, sometimes it was auburn. But she always kept it looking great!"

There was a nucleus of about three dozen girls who regularly worked Jarvis Street. They were well known to each other, and to the bouncers, barmen, and night managers of all the fleabags. They kept pretty much to this corner of the city, and as a rule didn't poach on the turf of the girls who worked Parkdale or the Mimico motels, in the city's west end lakeshore districts.

Every one of them was known to the police and had been picked up at one time or another for "Vag C," the catch-all vagrancy section of the Criminal Code hookers were charged with when they propositioned men for the purpose of prostitution. Tracy was no exception. She'd pleaded guilty to Vag C the year before and paid her hundred-dollar fine in cash without complaint – the cost of doing business – and was back on the street before court adjourned.

A half-dozen tricks a night, fifty bucks or more a time, depending on the john's sexual proclivities, no income tax. And that was just what Tracy turned six nights a week from suppertime to one or two in the morning. It didn't include what she made as a high-priced call girl during the daytime. One of the girls would tell us later that she'd been given a quick glance at Tracy's little black book, in which she kept the names, phone numbers, and descriptions of the sexual idiosyncrasies of a few dozen "professional" men about town, who regularly and gratefully paid big money for her attentions.

The book was not to be found among her personal effects. Where it went, neither Herm nor I could say, but we were assured that on any day of the week, many of those listed on its pages could be found dining elegantly on generous expense accounts at Winston's or the Board of Trade.

"You'll never guess where she lived," said Herm, who'd just hung up the phone after talking to the two 52 Division detectives who'd scooped her before.

"A little one-bedroom on Wellesley Street, according to this I.D.," I said, holding up a driver's licence.

"No, she just crashed there sometimes. And if she really knew a john well, she might even take him there."

"Where, then?"

"Those luxury apartments near Avenue Road and St. Clair."

Back at the hospital, Bill Urie had begun to talk to Marie-Louise, a petite West Indian girl who once did a double date with Tracy in the Westover.

"We always got lousy money at the Westover, and the johns there were real creeps," Marie-Louise said. "Anyway, she told me she had three kids, but one of them, a little boy, died of a tumour. She also told me she had another son in a private school. I think it's Upper Canada College – the one up near Avenue Road and St. Clair. She wanted to be close to him, but the kid doesn't know she hustled."

Anybody who gives currency to the expression "colder than a whore's heart" will have difficulty understanding the genuine sadness and grim resignation Bill Urie saw written on the faces of the women he spoke to that night. No matter what the world called them, they were still somebody's mother or daughter or sister, and damned few of them truly wanted to do what they were doing. Tonight they were mourning in their own fashion. Tracy's murder had shaken them up. With the exception of Bonnie, they were in a mood to talk to Urie – something hookers seldom did willingly with police officers.

"She was an easy-going, passive person," said Marie-Louise, who, in the course of Bill's interview, had nervously gnawed her fingernails to the quick. "She never used crude language, she was always exceptionally nice to her tricks, and she didn't go along with johns who wanted to do anything freaky or violent."

"The last I saw her was about 8:30 p.m.," said Phyllis, a striking brunette in her forties who worked days at a dry cleaner and nights hustling out of the Warwick to provide for herself and her two kids. "I was sitting in the coffee shop at the Warwick. The place was empty because everybody was in the bar watching the floor show. One of the waiters and two other girls came and sat with me, then Tracy came in and sat with us, too. She ordered a milk shake."

Of all the girls who spoke up that night, the one who'd known Tracy longest was Marie-Louise.

"There's something I need to ask you," Bill said to her.

"What is it?"

"The girl that was brought in . . . we need someone to identify her body. Do you think you can do that?"

She thought about it for a moment, then said with resolve, "I'll do it."

Bill knew what she was in for, but it couldn't be avoided. Sure enough, when she was taken into the alcove where the bloody corpse lay, poor Marie-Louise's resolve deserted her. She turned away in utter terror.

"Tracy. That's Tracy," she whispered.

Bill got her out of there as fast as he could. She had begun to tremble, and was in no shape to go anywhere but home, so before accompanying the body to the morgue, he arranged to have her dropped off outside her house in the west end of the city.

At about one in the morning, Herm and I entered the interview room on the second floor of 51 Division. There sat the bare-chested man, guarded by Alison Buchanan and Steve Craig.

"You guys can grab a coffee. Sergeant Lowe and I will take over here."

When the officers left the room, I introduced myself and Herm to the man, who sat in a chair by the window. Both legs of his faded work pants and the tops of his scuffed boots were blood-spattered, and his hands appeared to be gloved in dried blood.

I said, "The name in the hotel register says Wilson. Is that your real name?"

"No, it's Willsie, William Marvin Willsie. Sometimes I go by Robert Willsie, sometimes Wilson."

"How old are you?"

"Forty-seven."

"Ever been in trouble with the police before?"

"You could say so, yeah."

"Where do you live?"

"The Salvation Army hostel on Sherbourne Street."

"How long have you lived at the Sally Ann?"

"Not long. I move around a lot."

In fact, he had lived in numerous towns after leaving Windsor, where he was born. Along the way, he'd repeatedly landed in and out of prison on convictions for theft, break and enter, and forgery. Up until that night, however, he'd never been charged with any violent crime.

When I had obtained all the information I needed regarding Willsie's background, I put questions to him that dealt specifically with what had gone on between him and Tracy LaSalle.

"All I can say is I picked up a broad in the Warwick Hotel, and we ended up at Larry's Hideaway. I paid her fifty bucks, and then she tried to steal my last fifteen dollars. When I objected to her robbing me, she got mad.

"On the window ledge, there was a silver coat, and from under this she pulled out some kind of dagger. She came at me. To protect myself, I grabbed her by the wrist and took the knife away from her. We struggled . . ." His voice trailed off for a moment. Then he resumed his story: "I don't know what to say right now. I don't know what happened after that."

I asked him if there was anything else he wanted to tell us.

"Just this: If she hadn't tried to rob me, this wouldn't have happened."

We charged Willsie with second-degree murder and took the case to court. He was convicted and sentenced to life imprisonment, which meant he wouldn't get out for twenty-five years.

During the trial, the prosecuting crown called every one of the forty-six witnesses Herm and I had assembled. I'm sure, to the average law-abiding citizen unfamiliar with the arcane workings of the criminal courts, that sounds like a needlessly large number. They can be forgiven for presuming that the conviction and lifelong incarceration of a man who had repeatedly and remorselessly plunged a five-inch blade into the naked body of an unarmed woman ought to have been a foregone conclusion – a slam-dunk! But as a police officer, I had learned that when it comes to criminal court, there's no such thing as a foregone conclusion. Experience had taught me never to take anything for granted, and that every case must be proven beyond a shadow of a doubt – even when, as in this investigation, the accused had been caught literally red-handed.

Three years after he was sentenced, Willsie sought the advice of another lawyer, who launched a challenge to the conviction, claiming that when Tracy LaSalle swooned and fell backward on top of the knife, she gave *herself* the coup de grâce. Because the court reporter in the initial trial had died suddenly, no transcript of the initial court proceedings existed. Accordingly, Willsie was granted leave to appeal and a new trial was ordered.

During the second trial, the crown was unable to prove, through pathological evidence, that any one of the four savage wounds deliberately inflicted on Tracy by Willsie had been the one to kill her. At least two of them *could* have caused her death, but it could not conclusively be demonstrated that any of them actually *did* kill her. Willsie was ultimately convicted of the lesser charge of manslaughter. In his wisdom, the judge saw fit to give him eighteen months in reformatory.

Did Herm and I like the verdict? No. Did we accept it? Absolutely.

Both of us understood that it was not up to us, or any other police officer for that matter, to act as judge, jury, and jailer. Whether or not we agreed with the court's decision, we knew we had done our job to the best of our ability. We'd collected the evidence, interviewed and prepared the witnesses, dealt fairly with the accused and compassionately with the victim's family, briefed the crown attorney, and then we had presented our case to the court.

For better or worse, the court had spoken.

The final day of the second trial was on our day off. When it was all over, Herm and I permitted ourselves a rare extravagance. We walked over to a local bar called The Witness Box. When the waiter placed our drinks on the table, Herm hoisted his glass and said, "We did our job, partner. Nobody could have asked us to do more."

We clinked glasses and watched in bemused silence the comings and goings of Toronto's legal luminaries.

8

The Obsession

*M*ost homicides are crimes of passion – compulsive acts carried out *by people who often have no criminal record. In the aftermath, it is frequently the passionate killer who is the most horrified and inconsolable, the one who wishes that above all else he could relive those horrible ten or twenty seconds when all reason was abandoned to blind fury.*

Ryan Kelso* is boiling with rage and the bile that erupts from his belly scorches his esophagus. He has seen the silver Corvette Stingray parked behind Emily's apartment, again. He knows what's going on inside, and it's going to stop – for good.

He can't get his key to work in Emily's apartment door, but that doesn't stop him. He works the bolt action of the Lee-Enfield .303, ramming a shell into the chamber, then points the barrel of the high-powered rifle directly at the lock and pulls the trigger. In one

* The names of the people involved in this tragedy have been changed for reasons of privacy.

thunderous explosion the bullet obliterates the cylinder, piercing the half-inch-thick deadbolt and sending it ripping sideways through the wooden door, where it hangs like an amputated thumb from the doorjamb. Vicious shards of shrapnel from the disintegrated lock hiss through the apartment, gouging furniture and picture frames, perforating wooden moulding and human flesh. The force of the concussion sends the door swinging violently inward against the wall, embedding the brass handle in the lath and plaster.

Ryan stands at the threshold glaring down the hall to the bathroom, twenty feet away. He sees Emily rise naked and dripping wet from the bathtub. Her face and shoulders bear scores of pock marks from the flying slivers of metal. A tiny bead of blood begins to glisten from each puncture. She is surprised and stupefied by the suddenness and ferocity of Ryan's intrusion.

The Australian is with her, as Ryan knew he would be. He and Emily have been sipping wine by candlelight while bathing. She steps out of the tub and begins walking towards Ryan. In a pitiful attempt to shield herself, she holds her hands outstretched, fingers spread and rigid, the way a little girl might if someone were playfully spraying her with a garden hose. But there is no glee in her face, no mischief. Instead, it is contorted in a silent, anguished scream.

"Why can't I hear her?" Ryan wonders, then realizes the gunshot has deafened him. The only thing he can hear — sense, really, and only deep inside his rioting brain — is his own uneven breathing, which comes in wracking sobs.

No matter, he's in no mood to listen to anybody now — not Emily, not the Australian, not anybody. Too late for that. He tells himself they're going to pay an awful price for what they've put him through!

He works the rifle's bolt action again, and while Emily pantomimes in terror, he raises the gun, sights her in, and shoots her clean through the heart. Though she's already dead, she somehow manages to stay on her feet. So he works the action and fires again, leaving a second nickel-sized hole in her chest, this one knocking her to the bathroom floor. As she lies writhing, Ryan pumps two more shells into her. Now she is motionless, dead eyes staring blankly down the hall.

The Australian stays seated in the bathtub. He looks once in Ryan's direction, then snaps his head away, covering his face with his hands. He knows Ryan has come for him too, and that there's nowhere to hide. The walls, the ceiling, and the tub itself have been splattered with Emily's blood and scraps of her liver and lungs. So has every part of his body that is exposed above the water.

Twice more Ryan ratchets shells into the rifle's chamber and fires. Both bullets tear through the man's right side below his armpit. He slumps forward and to his left until his forehead dips into the water, which quickly turns bright red. He too has been shot dead through the heart.

Still clutching the rifle, Ryan turns and stumbles from the apartment.

It is a warm August evening in 1975. Most of the tenants in this modest but well-kept apartment building overlooking the Humber River have their windows open to catch the early evening breeze off Lake Ontario. The young man who lives in the apartment next to Emily's has just arrived home from work, and is trying to decide what to make for supper. Absently, he glances out his front window to the sidewalk, where he sees Ryan Kelso, the man who used to live with Emily, walk by. He watches as Kelso enters the building. Only his shoulders and head are visible as he passes the window. This can't be good, the young man thinks;

she kicked him out a couple of weeks ago. There's going to be trouble.

Five seconds later, no more than that, the calm of the young man's small and orderly apartment is shattered by a loud blast. And five seconds after that, he hears a series of blasts in rapid succession. Five? Six? Who can say? Gunfire is not something he has ever heard thundering through his quiet apartment building. This can't be happening, not here!

He returns to the matter of what he ought to prepare for supper. Think! Think hard! What am I going to eat? For just a moment, he harbours vague thoughts of calling the police to tell them he heard shots. But he convinces himself they'd never believe him. They'd laugh at him, or get angry and say he was crazy; nobody shoots a gun off in the city. No, he would stay right there and mind his own business. Whatever was going on, it had nothing to do with him. Besides, he didn't really *know* anything was wrong.

He doesn't call. But a pensioner who lives in a house across the street from the apartment building does call the police. He and his wife saw a man with a gun.

Approximately fifteen minutes after Ryan Kelso blasted his way into the apartment and slaughtered Emily and her lover, Constable Norm Vanderburgh of 11 Division has arrived outside the building with his partner, a rookie by the name of Greg Higgins. They were dispatched after an elderly couple saw a slightly built man in his mid-twenties with collar-length hair run from the building to a beige station wagon. He was carrying a rifle – or a shotgun, they're not really sure – which he tossed through an open window on the passenger side of the car before running to the driver's side, climbing behind the wheel, and speeding down the street, tires squealing, rear end fishtailing.

"And then, what did he do?"

"Like I said, my wife and I were sitting right here on the verandah as he tore past in his car. And he looked right at us. I'm sure he knew we'd seen him. Isn't that right, dear?"

"Yes, he looked right at us. Saw us both."

"Would you recognize him if you saw him again, ma'am?"

"Of course, officer."

"And you, sir?"

"Sure I would."

The officers cross the street to the building, unsure of which apartment to approach, unaware that shots had been fired. Norm Vanderburgh sees a young man standing at one of the windows and motions to him to open the front door. The man complies, and as the officers step across the threshold, their palates taste the acrid sweetness of burnt gunpowder.

They draw their revolvers.

"Down there," the young man says, and points in the direction of Emily's apartment.

The officers close in on the apartment door and notice the hole in the lock and the severed deadbolt hanging uselessly from the jamb. Vanderburgh plucks the cheap departmental-issue ballpoint pen from a slender pouch sewn into the breast pocket of his uniform shirt and, placing the blunt end on the very top right corner of the door, cautiously pushes it open.

Straight ahead of him, the body of a young woman is sprawled on its right side across the bathroom floor. Eyes devoid of all expression stare directly at him, and the officer half expects her to stand. Behind her, and still in the bathtub, slumps the body of a man. Taking great care where he steps, Vanderburgh moves far enough into the apartment to assure himself there's no one hiding there. To Greg Higgins he says, "You stand at the door, and don't let anybody in." Higgins has been a police officer for all of a year and a half. He does exactly what he's told.

Vanderburgh turns to the young man who had opened the front door and asks to use his phone. After calling his station to inform the staff sergeant what he was dealing with, he asks the young man to explain what had gone on in the apartment next door.

"And after you saw this guy you call Kelso walk up to the building, what happened?"

"Then I heard what sounded like a gunshot. I mean I didn't really think it was a gun. Who'd be stupid enough to fire off one of those around here? And then I heard five or six more, I'm not sure."

"And what did you do then?"

"Well, then I thought I'd just start making supper. And I think I put on some music. Yeah, I bought a new Stan Kenton album last week, and I put that on while I tried to figure out what to eat."

"And did you see or hear anything after that?"

"No, not until I saw you pull up outside in the police car and talk to those people across the street. That's when I let you into the building."

"All right, then. Thank you, sir. Detectives from the Homicide Squad are on their way here. They'll no doubt want to talk to you later. By the way, it doesn't look like you got around to making your supper."

"Supper? No, I guess I didn't. Funny, eh?"

Vanderburgh and Higgins were joined at the scene within minutes by 11 Division investigators John Gomez and Peter Hymers, who found a few more neighbours who either heard the shots or saw the gunman fleeing.

One man had seen the beige station wagon pull up in front of the building, and the driver fiddling with something in the front seat. The witness said the man seemed to be assembling something. "This went on for a few minutes," the witness reported. "Then he got out of the car and it was then that I noticed that he had a large, greenish sleeve-type case. It looked awfully big to me. He put it under his arm and walked towards the building." A gun sheath was later found on the hallway floor outside the apartment.

It was about 7:50 p.m. when the call came through to the Homicide office, where I was working alone. Fifteen minutes later, I was walking up the front steps of the apartment building. It was a beautiful evening, but instead of enjoying the rosy Toronto sunset, the dozens of people sitting on their front steps up and down the street were grimly transfixed by the comings and goings of ambulances, police cars, and television news vans. Word had gotten around that the police were investigating a double shooting, and that the gunman was still on the loose.

His description and details of the car he was seen driving had, by this time, been broadcast to all Metro police officers, as well as to officers in surrounding areas, including the Ontario Provincial Police.

I was told by Constable Higgins that the coroner had preceded my arrival, and that he had already pronounced both people dead. Young Higgins was very precise as he briefed me, making certain that he covered every detail, eager to make a good impression on a senior officer. Rookie police officers live in dread of "shitting in their nest," as the saying goes. And in the course of a major investigation, which all homicide cases are, the possibilities of screwing up royally are virtually endless. Greg Higgins needn't have worried. No one got into that apartment who wasn't supposed to be there. And that included a nosy acting deputy chief who showed up – a throwback to much earlier days when "heavies" traipsed into murder scenes sucking on cheap cigars. I was confident, as I stood talking to the young officer, that nothing inside the apartment had been disturbed.

Higgins conducted himself like an old pro. And so did Norm

Vanderburgh, whom I detailed to set up a temporary command and communication post in the apartment of the young man next door, who by then had given up on supper completely.

My arrival at the apartment was followed almost immediately by that of George Barrett and Tom Jeffries, two old hands from Ident who had worked with me on many homicide investigations. Together, we surveyed the scene: Once past the door, with its obliterated lock and deadbolt, we found a number of spent shell casings and bullets, as well as one live round. On the living room wall facing the door, we found two holes – one made by a bullet, the other by a piece of shrapnel. Wooden splinters from the door littered the hallway floor leading to the bathroom that held the two lifeless bodies.

The bathtub and one wall bore the marks of bullets that had ripped through the bodies of both victims and buried themselves there. One slug had ricocheted upward, shattering a ceiling light fixture and showering both victims with jagged blades of glass. This likely was a bullet that had torn through the bathroom door.

The body of twenty-year-old Emily Ward lay atop a blood-soaked pile of men's and women's clothing. The couple had apparently stepped out of them beside the tub before bathing. The body of a man, whom we would soon identify as twenty-eight-year-old Richard Tucker, sat bent over at the waist in about five inches of blood and bathwater, his right hand shielding his face. Both had bullet wounds on their upper bodies.

I left George and Tom in charge of the apartment, knowing they would do their usual thorough job of collecting every scrap of physical evidence there was to be found, and of fingerprinting, measuring, and photographing the scene. When the Ident boys had finished scouring the apartment – a job that would take them at least two days – Sergeant Joe

Veater would go to work measuring everything in the place in order to prepare a scale drawing of the scene. Joe was a professional draftsman whose meticulous drawings were crucial to the crown's case, since photographs of homicide victims are seldom admitted into evidence. Pictures of murder victims are almost always gruesome and are regarded by the court (to say nothing of defence lawyers) as inflammatory and prejudicial to the accused. Of course, most of the crown attorneys I worked with – people like Bob McGee, Norm Matusiak, and Paul Culver – became expert at using Joe's drawings and testimony to identify for the jury the exact location of this droplet of blood or that shell casing, and the positioning of the body. More times than not, Tom Veater's scale drawing of a murder scene was the first piece of evidence called for by the jury when it began its deliberations.

With the scene taken care of, I began to organize the search for the gunman, now known to be twenty-five-year-old Ryan Kelso, a sometime labourer, sometime truck driver, and former lover of Emily Ward.

The following morning, I attended the postmortem examinations of both victims. I also took the unusual, though not unheard of, step of inviting a firearms expert from the crime lab to witness the autopsies. Over the years, I had found that the presence of forensic scientists and technicians at certain postmortems could be very useful. Invariably, they discovered that they could compose a much more accurate picture of what had gone on at a crime scene whenever they were allowed to attend. This, of course, was usually reflected in the quality of their testimony, which the court found extremely helpful.

The autopsy confirmed that the deaths of both victims came as a direct result of being shot through the heart, and that massive injury had been caused to most of their vital organs. Even if their hearts had not been struck, the .303 slugs that had rampaged through the chest cavities of both victims had so horribly mangled everything in their paths that neither person could possibly have survived the shooting. The Lee-Enfield .303 is as lethal a killing tool as can be found in any gun rack. If a bullet from one of these weapons strikes even a limb of its quarry, death is the probable result, because the slug will twist erratically and deep into the body, lacerating muscle, severing arteries, and shattering bone.

That afternoon, I went to Old City Hall and obtained a warrant to arrest Ryan Kelso on two counts of murder.

With the help of investigators from 11 Division, I began to question those who knew both the victims and their killer. I discovered that Kelso and Ward had lived together common law for four years. In recent months, she had begun to question their relationship. She told Kelso that she saw no future in it and wanted out. He wouldn't hear of it, and they fought. When she asked him to leave their apartment, he reluctantly complied. But when he suspected that she was seeing Tucker, he angrily told her she was making a big mistake, and that he was going to move back in with her.

Witnesses told me that Kelso was consumed by jealousy and had descended into a deep depression. Others told me that a chronic stress-related stomach problem, for which he had been receiving medical treatment, had flared up again, robbing him of sleep and the will to eat. After only a week as a deckhand on one of the bulk carriers plying the Great Lakes, he had quit his job and returned to Toronto, where all he did was mope around.

Convinced he was falling apart, and that it was all Emily's fault, he approached every one of her friends and relatives in an effort to enlist their support. Curiously, the most sympathetic ear belonged to Emily's mother, Roberta, an attractive forty-two-year-old, who had taken Kelso in when Emily kicked him out. Friends and relatives thought it strange that Roberta should share a place with Kelso, especially since he routinely ridiculed her – both to her face and behind her back. About a week before the murders, he helped her move into a flat half a mile west of Emily's apartment. From there, it was easy for Kelso to keep an eye on his former lover – and her new boyfriend, the cocky Australian who drove the silver Corvette Stingray.

The day Kelso moved Roberta, he drove to Barrie to stay with some friends. She followed the day after, and was in the room when Kelso tried to talk his host into buying his entire gun collection. He claimed he wanted rid of them, and that he intended to buy a train ticket to Vancouver with the money. He felt he had to get out of Toronto. The pressure of knowing Emily was just a few blocks away with another man was eating him up, he said.

According to numerous friends we spoke to, the troubles between Emily and Ryan Kelso went back a long way. He had a temper, a small collection of firearms, and a penchant for pointing them fully loaded at people who crossed him. We learned that he had pointed a loaded weapon at Emily's father – Roberta's estranged husband – and at a woman with whom he had lived five years before. That time, a four-year-old girl had also been in the room. Somehow, Kelso had managed to avoid being charged criminally, and was able to keep his guns.

It seemed to most of Emily's and Ryan's friends and acquaintances that in the days leading up to the shootings, if he wasn't talking about the sad shape he was in, he was talking about guns. Four weeks before the shootings, Kelso went to the home of a woman he had known for eight years, who had befriended Emily and knew about the rocky state of her relationship with Ryan. In her statement to me, the woman said that Kelso told her in one breath that he wanted rid of his guns, and in the next that he was interested in buying an automatic pistol "in case me and my buddy want to go hunting."

"What would you hunt with an automatic pistol?" she'd asked.

"Corvette Stingrays."

She changed the subject.

The remainder of that weekend and all day Monday were spent interviewing those who knew the victims and their killer. All were cooperative. If Ryan had shown up at any of their homes, I felt certain they'd find a way to tip me off. I was sure Kelso had fled the city and had likely headed somewhere up north.

Early Tuesday afternoon, I got a call. At the other end of the line was a well-known criminal lawyer. He'd been contacted by Ryan Kelso, who had been following news reports about himself for the past couple of days. He knew we had a warrant for his arrest, and after talking to the lawyer, had decided to give himself up.

At five-thirty that afternoon, the lawyer walked into the Homicide office. With him was a frightened, skinny, pale young man with blue eyes and stringy brown hair and a mustache. The lawyer introduced his client to me and to Herm Lowe, who would work with me to the completion of the investigation. As soon as the introductions were dispensed with, I put my hand on Kelso's shoulder and placed him under arrest, cautioning him on two counts of murder punishable by life imprisonment.

"My lawyer told me you'd do that," was his response.

"Do you understand the charges, Ryan?" I asked.

"Yes, I understand."

For the next few minutes Kelso spoke privately with his counsel, who told him we'd be asking him for his cooperation in finding the gun he used in the shooting, as well as all the others he owned. The decision to cooperate was his alone. Then the lawyer left the office.

I entered the small interview room, where Kelso sat nervously smoking a cigarette.

"Well, Ryan, is there anything you want to tell Sergeant Lowe and me?"

"Yes, there is."

And for the next hour, he dictated a complete account of the relationship he'd had with Emily Ward, which had ended so tragically and violently four days before. He told us he'd met Emily at a beach some years ago, and that after a brief period of dating, they had decided to live together in an apartment close to her parents in the city's west end. She soon became pregnant, but because they were struggling financially, the couple decided to give the child up for adoption.

At about this time, Emily's parents separated, and the couple looked for somewhere else to live. In the four years that they lived together, Ryan struggled in various jobs and with his own business, which eventually went bankrupt. Sensing that their relationship was drifting, Ryan tried to talk Emily into seeking professional marriage counselling, but she wanted none of it. Instead, she wanted a change of scene.

One afternoon, when the couple was taking a tour around Toronto harbour aboard one of the tall ships that provide sightseeing trips, another passenger by the name of Richard Tucker began flirting with Emily. She was flattered, and naturally kept her feelings from Ryan, who she knew would be jealous. She began to meet secretly with Richard, and her relationship with Ryan continued to deteriorate. Eventually Emily asked Ryan to move out.

Kelso told Herm and me that he hadn't suspected that Emily had been seeing anybody else until about two weeks before the shootings. After a marathon argument one evening, he had returned to their apartment at five the following morning to discover that she wasn't there. He rummaged around the bedroom and found a letter Emily had written to her sister in which she said she'd been seeing Tucker, and that this had been going on for some time before she and Kelso had broken up.

Later that morning, he called her at work and exploded. There were accusations and counter-accusations and, to make matters worse, she told him he couldn't return to the apartment because Tucker's mother, who was visiting from Australia, was staying there. This sent Kelso into a dangerous tailspin.

In the days that followed, he tried to get someone – *anyone* – to buy his guns. He wanted enough money for a train ticket to Vancouver, where he hoped he could make a new start. A friend expressed real interest, but was having trouble scraping up the money.

"By Friday morning, I was starting to feel the pressure bad. I phoned the guy who was interested in buying my guns and told him I wanted to sell them so I could get as far away from Toronto as fast as I could."

On the Friday evening, he drove past Emily's apartment, and there in the parking lot was Tucker's silver Corvette Stingray. He parked his car and entered the building. Standing outside Emily's apartment, he could hear her and the Australian laughing and talking, having a good time. That is the very moment when Ryan Kelso came undone. The humiliation of the past several weeks was too much to bear. If he couldn't have her, nobody could!

He ran back to his car and drove to a nearby sporting goods store, where he bought a box of .303 shells. He already had his guns in the car, presumably so that he could turn them over, should his friend come up with the money.

He was sitting outside the apartment building in his car minutes later. Reaching under the back seat, he pulled out the disassembled rifle and began putting it together. He grabbed a handful of shells and crammed them into the gun's magazine.

"I blew the door open. I saw Emily and him, and they were both naked. I was so shocked. Emily had gotten out of the tub, and I was mainly looking at her. I don't think I even aimed the gun. *Bang!* I fired. I don't know how many times I fired. I know that I was deaf with the noise, and I just fired and fired and fired!"

Reliving the shootings, he trembled and his voice cracked with grief. I waited until he regained composure. He went on to tell us about his helter-skelter flight from the city, and about pulling into a gas station near Lake Simcoe where he couldn't hear a single word the kid who filled the tank was saying because his ears were still ringing. He described the dusty country road where he searched for a place to rid himself of the bullets and the gun.

"It was dusk, and getting pretty dark. I took what was left of the box of shells and chucked them out the window while I was driving up the dirt road. I was having a devil of a time trying to think, and especially to hear. I stopped somewhere and got out. I threw the gun into what I thought was a good section of bush."

"Is there anything else you want to tell me, Ryan?"

"Just this: from whatever time this whole thing started, up to the moment it happened, I had no intentions of shooting anybody."

The next day, Herm and I got Kelso out of the Old City Hall cells and drove him north towards Barrie in search of the murder weapon. While Herm drove, I sat in the back seat of the cruiser talking with Kelso, from whose wrists I had removed the handcuffs. Once out of the city, we stopped at a roadside diner intending to grab a bite to eat. Kelso held out his wrists, believing I was going to place the cuffs on them again.

"Tell me, Ryan, will handcuffs be necessary?" I asked.

He looked at me in utter disbelief that I was prepared to trust him.

"Thank you" was all he could manage while choking back tears.

We chose a corner booth away from the other patrons, who were none the wiser about our identity or purpose for passing through. Over lunch, Kelso unburdened his heart. He was horrified by what he'd done, and his remorse for the killings was genuine and absolute.

After a search of several hours, we found the bullets and the Lee-Enfield .303, as well as the remainder of his gun collection. Kelso also took us to the densely wooded corner of an abandoned farm where he had purposely tried to hide his car by driving it deep into a thick stand of saplings. While many of them had been snapped off as the car rolled over them, many more had sprung back up, effectively concealing the car from view beyond a distance of fifty feet in any direction.

Five months later, there was a trial. Ryan Kelso was found guilty on both counts of murder, and was sentenced to two concurrent life terms in prison.

Herm and I followed Kelso downstairs to the cells after the verdict was announced. We were afraid he might attempt to commit suicide – not because the verdict and the life term came as a shock to him, but because he was overcome by guilt.

"You can't undo what you've done, Ryan," I said.

"But I don't know how I'm going to live with it, either."

As we stood facing each other, with the bars of his cell between us, he confided in Herm and me: "I decided after I gave myself up that I wouldn't get out of jail alive, but now I've changed my mind."

He told us he was going to try to put his life back together again. He also told us he would never get over Emily.

I strongly doubt that he ever got over Emily, or that he will ever be able to forgive himself for killing her and Tucker. But something happened years later that gave me hope that he might be trying to make a new life for himself.

It was on the occasion of my appointment as Chief of the Metropolitan Toronto Police Force in October 1989, a role I had filled on an interim basis since the previous July. Among the scores of letters of congratulations that I received was one postmarked Kingston, Ontario. It said, in part, "Though we met when I was charged with murder, you treated me fairly and with compassion. You always told me the truth. I knew then that you would accomplish good things, and now I'm pleased to see that you've been promoted to the rank of Chief of Police."

The letter was unsigned, but I've always suspected that its author was Ryan Kelso.

9

The Baker's Dozen

*M*any times during my years on the Homicide Squad, I was struck *by the role played by chance in the lives of those involved in the cases I investigated. The often sinister, sometimes funny, and always improbable collision of circumstances that connected total strangers never ceased to amaze me. Rarely, however, did happenstance contrive to produce the kind of deadly results described in the case that follows.*

The woman's fully clothed body lay sprawled across the bed. She'd been strangled to death. Pantyhose had been knotted around her throat and drawn tight, choking the life out of her. It had taken her several seconds to succumb, and throughout her agonizing ordeal, she had flailed about helplessly. In the course of her death throes she had blindly flung out an arm, sending a bedside lamp crashing to the floor, breaking its neck and caving in its cheap cardboard shade.

Ligature strangulation, the pathologists call it. A horrible way to die, the face contorted in a grimacing mask, eyes bugged out, tongue protruding between bared teeth, lurid purple blotches on the forehead, cheeks, and neck where blood, dammed up at the gullet, is trapped in mid-flow. With nowhere to go, it collects in dark pools beneath the surface of the skin.

It was her husband who'd killed her before running out the front door of the tiny wartime frame house, smack-dab into a neighbour who moments before had heard the screaming and was hurrying up the driveway. This was not the first time neighbours had had to intervene in the couple's battles.

"I killed her! I killed her!" the husband screamed. "I'm going to jump off the bluffs!"

The neighbour watched in shock as the distraught man clambered behind the wheel of his car and roared off down the street. The neighbour ran into the house, scrambling from room to room and calling the victim's name until he found the body. He clawed desperately at the nylon noose, but it was wrapped so tightly around the woman's neck that it cut into the skin. He worked feverishly, but in vain, to loosen the knot. Weeping with frustration, he ran to the kitchen and called the police.

Uniformed officers from 43 Division were on the scene in minutes, and so was an ambulance, but it was too late. Nothing could be done for her.

George Thompson and I got to the house at one that afternoon. On the way over, we'd kept our eyes open for the car the man had been seen driving. A description had been broadcast by the first officer on the scene, who had also found a photograph of the suspect; the photo was rushed to Headquarters, where Ident was busy making copies of it for distribution to all Scarborough units. Already every police officer the radio room could spare was combing the parks and beaches along the eight-mile stretch of Scarborough Bluffs, which tower above Lake Ontario from Victoria Park Avenue to Morningside Avenue.

We got word that someone answering the man's description had been spotted in Bluffers Park about fifteen minutes after the neighbour had seen him fleeing the house. A primary school teacher and a gaggle of grade two kids had encountered a man walking along a lakeside path. When the teacher greeted him, pleasantly remarking what a fine day it was, he looked at her blankly and, in a matter-of-fact tone, said, "Fine day? Yes, I guess it is. But I just killed my wife, and now I'm going to jump off the bluffs."

She didn't take him seriously – at least, not right away. It wasn't until she got back to the school several minutes later that she considered that what the man had said to her might indeed have been true, and not just a bad joke. Feeling somewhat foolish, she called the police switchboard operator, who immediately patched her through to the station duty officer at 43 Division.

Now we had a starting point.

Murder suspect or not, the man's safety became our primary focus. George and I sealed the tiny house, intending to return later, and took charge of what amounted to a search and rescue operation that would come to involve hundreds of people.

We got to Bluffers Park a little before three o'clock. It had been approximately two hours since the man had been sighted, and we were concerned that he might have carried out his threat, though a careful street-by-street search revealed no sign of his car, and none of the cab companies had brought a fare matching his description to that part of the lakeshore.

George made a quick assessment of the situation and came to the conclusion that we needed two things in a hurry before nightfall, about six hours hence: an aerial view of the bluffs and a thorough search of the churning waters beneath them. When George Thompson had a job to do, nothing could stand in his way. There wasn't a vehicle, indeed a conveyance of any kind, that he would not commandeer. Nor was there a person, regardless of occupation or station in life, whom he would not conscript – shanghai, if necessary – to get the job done. Never had I worked with a more resourceful or tenaciously determined police officer.

He stood at the very lip of the bluffs, scanning the water with one hand shading his eyes. Then he turned and marched purposefully over to where I stood giving instructions to a uniformed sergeant in charge of a contingent of men.

"What we need here, Bill, is a chopper!"

"You mean a helicopter? Where the hell are we gonna get one of those?"

"Get on the blower to CKEY. They've got one we can use."

Before ten minutes had passed, radio station CKEY's traffic helicopter was noisily hunkering down on the grass plateau above the bluffs, its whirlwind sending a half-dozen police hats hurtling over the brink and into the lake three hundred feet below. When the big blade finally drooped to a stop, the pilot and his lone passenger, a radio news reporter, hopped out and stood by the bubble. George strode over, shook the pilot's hand, and thanked him for coming so quickly. "We need to put a police officer up there in that machine with you," he stated matter-of-factly. Then George turned around and pointed his finger at a dumbfounded young uniformed man who was still grieving the loss of his hat and said, "Officer, I want you to go aloft with the pilot. Make sure you keep an eye peeled for our man."

Well, I'm sure the kid's jaw must have dropped a foot. He could scarcely believe what he'd heard. He looked doubtfully at the helicopter.

"You want me to go up in *that* thing, Sarge?"

I could hardly blame him. Though it had been provided free, and at a moment's notice, the ungainly flying machine had the look of an overgrown eggbeater.

With one eyebrow arched, George snapped his head around and impaled the young officer with a withering stare. Immediately, the kid got the message and stepped smartly, though ashen-faced, towards the chopper.

"Which side do I sit on?" he asked glumly.

"Mine," offered the reporter, who was clearly displeased at having been sidelined, just when he thought he'd be in on a terrific scoop. The pilot cast him an apologetic glance, then climbed in behind the controls. The engine whined. Slowly, the propeller built up speed until, with a sudden rush of power, the rickety little contraption lifted off the rippling grass and was carried away on the wind like a spinning maple key.

Immensely satisfied now that his airborne surveillance team was aloft, George turned his attention to the flotilla of pleasure craft and Harbour Police boats that had been hastily assembled at his request, and which was, at that very moment, speeding eastward towards us along the coast from the city. Over the next several hours, they would string themselves out at regular intervals several feet offshore and drag the lake bottom directly beneath the bluffs.

Now, to the ground troops.

Our company of fifty or so full-time police constables, who were beating the bushes along the crest of the bluffs, had been augmented by twice as many auxiliary officers – unpaid civilians in uniform, from all walks of life, who worked a minimum of thirty-two hours a month and helped regular officers perform an array of duties, including search and rescue operations such as this. They were under the command of one of the most capable and enterprising men I'd ever met. James Carnegie had built Metro's Auxiliary Police Force almost single-handedly, one volunteer at a time. And, as the influential Chairman of the Metropolitan Toronto Board of Trade, he wouldn't hesitate to use his powerful connections to call upon assistance. He was one of those people you wanted in your corner when things got tight.

As dusk approached, the subject of our search had yet to be found. If we didn't locate him soon, we'd be forced to continue looking in the dark, and run the risk of losing one or more of our searchers over the bluffs. Anticipating that we might find ourselves in just such a predicament, George had earlier asked me to phone the Canadian Forces Base at Trenton to request the use of their arc lights. It would be one of scores of times during my career when I would request and receive the able and willing assistance of Canada's Armed Forces. And every time I had anything to do with them, they carried out their duties with precision and professionalism.

As soon as it grew dark enough, a command was given, and for miles along the Scarborough Bluffs, night turned suddenly into day. A salty old duty inspector who'd dropped by to mooch some coffee and a doughnut turned to me and said, "Who does Thompson think he is, for cryin' out loud, Busby Berkeley? This ain't a search and rescue operation, it's a fuckin' pageant!"

Just then, George stuck his head out of the police cruiser that he'd been using as a mobile command post, a triumphant expression on his face. "The dog's on the way!"

"What dog?" asked the duty inspector, grumpy as hell that no one had consulted him.

"The one from Barrie OPP. He'll be here in about an hour."

"Dogs! Now he's got dogs, for Pete's sake." The man shook his head in disgust.

The OPP dog was a beautiful German shepherd, and the first thing it did, when its handler let it out of the back of the OPP station wagon, was saunter over to where the DI sat in his cruiser and lift its leg on the left front tire. The inspector fixed the handler with a malevolent stare, then put his car in gear and drove slowly away.

Thank goodness, for what happened next would have sent the DI right through the roof.

"Take me to where the subject was last seen," said the dog man, all business. Whereupon he and his canine sidekick were guided to the point on the path at which the grade two teacher had seen and talked to the suspect. The dog eagerly sniffed the ground and began to whine and then to yelp. It strained at its lead, hopping on its hind legs at the end of its tether. The magnificent brute practically turned itself inside-out trying to get free so it could charge into the abundant undergrowth after the fugitive.

George was inspired!

"We're in business now, Bill!" he enthused. "That dog's primed. Watch this!"

The handler reached down to release the clip that held his dog. At that very instant, there suddenly appeared a silver-grey flash in the tall grass to the left of the path. A rabbit! It caught the dog's eye, and before anyone could do anything about it, he plunged after it. The chase was on.

"Come!" barked the dog handler, but the animal was deaf to the command. "Come!" he barked again. But it was no use, that damned dog was on a mission!

A dozen times, with ears flat to its head and pink tongue flapping crazily out the side of its mouth, the dog criss-crossed the path ahead of us in hot pursuit of its prey. And each time it did, one of us dove after it. We must have made a curious procession indeed: the rabbit chased by the police dog, which was pursued by its handler, who was followed by an exceedingly ruffled George Thompson and, bringing up the rear, me. Thanks to CFB Trenton – and to the profound delight of scores of footsore police officers, amused lakeside residents, and news reporters – the entire ridiculous spectacle was lit up like a Hollywood set.

There's no denying it, our plans for running our suspect to ground, with the aid of one of the OPP's finest, were in complete disarray. With all dignity gone, the mortified dog handler, who had failed repeatedly to snatch his animal's collar as it passed, resorted to yelling – bleating, actually – at his rampaging partner:

"C'mere, you dumb sonofabitch! Heel! Heel, I said!"

And finally, in utter exasperation, "Come back here, you stupid, flea-bitten arsehole. Yer chasin' a friggin' rabbit!"

Now, it would have been unfair to lay all the blame at the feet of the poor animal. I'm sure that in his small doggy mind, he believed – truly believed – that we wanted him to *get that rabbit!* And that's what he was going to do, even if it killed him.

Which it almost did.

Not quite as nimble as its long-eared quarry, the huge German shepherd very nearly lost its footing and would have skidded over the edge of the bluffs to its death had its handler not made one last desperate lunge for its choke-chain as the frenzied animal rushed past.

"Thank goodness that's over," the flustered dog man said, as he breathlessly re-attached the lead.

One look at George told me he was peeved. For the first time since I'd known him, his hair was mussed, his tie was askew, and there was the slightest trace of perspiration on his upper lip. Worse still, there was a small amount of mud on the shin of one trouser leg. For a long moment, he glowered at the hapless dog man, who stood sheepishly looking at the ground, then turned to me and said, "C'mon, Bill. Next time we'll call the RCMP."

We didn't find our murder suspect that night, so George and I called off the search and headed back to the modest little house where the homicide had taken place. There, we spent the next eight hours with a team from Ident, photographing and measuring the scene and collecting physical evidence. It was four o'clock on Saturday morning by the time we got back to Headquarters and prepared a summary of the events that had taken place over the previous sixteen hours. I do not recall that our report made any mention whatsoever of the rabbit.

Since the postmortem was scheduled for eleven o'clock that morning, we decided to go home and grab a few hours' sleep. I don't know about George, but I had trouble dropping off. Jean told me later that I seemed to be laughing in my sleep.

In what seemed like no time at all, we were at 86 Lombard Street taking notes on the woman's autopsy. By the time we had secured all of the necessary exhibits from the pathologist and completed our paperwork on the murder, it was 8:00 p.m. I was exhausted. George, on the other hand, looked as though he were ready to go dancing. I often wondered how he was able to put in the punishing hours we worked in Homicide and still look like he'd just stepped out of a spa.

It was now more than thirty hours since the murder suspect's neighbour had seen him run from the house, and we still hadn't had a sniff of him, so to speak. While every division in Metro kept an eye out for him, George and I decided to try for a decent night's sleep and start fresh at ten the next morning, which was Sunday.

About an hour before we were to start work, I got a call at home from the station duty officer at 51 Division, a tough police station in a bare-knuckled neighbourhood of Toronto known as Cabbagetown.

"I've got a confession to make, Sergeant McCormack."

And when I asked him to explain, he told me that earlier that morning he'd taken a call from a man who told him he'd been walking through St. James Cemetery, on Parliament Street north of Wellesley, when he'd come across a dead body.

"You got nothin' better to do than play silly bugger on the phone?" demanded the officer, who then slammed down the receiver and went back to sorting parking tickets.

"Who was that?" asked his staff sergeant.

"Some peckerhead thought we should know there's a dead body in St. James Cemetery."

The staff sergeant shook his head and chuckled. Crank calls were nothing new in this division, which was home to a large number and variety of characters – many of whom were known to tipple before breakfast, let alone before noon.

The phone rang again, about two minutes later.

"Honest, there's a dead man in St. James Cemetery. I'm tellin' yuh!"

"And I'm tellin' you, if you call here again, I'll find out where you are and come down there and twist you into a bottle. Now, bugger off!"

Again, the station duty man slammed down the receiver.

Ten minutes passed. The phone rang again.

"Don't hang up! Don't hang up! I know you think I'm shittin' yuh, but I'm not. There's a guy hung himself at the bottom end of St. James Cemetery. And that's the God's truth!"

Sure enough, when the uniformed officer patrolling in the area of the cemetery checked out the caller's story, he found a man hanging from the limb of a tree. He was quite dead. And though the man's face had been horribly distorted and discoloured, due to ligature strangulation, one look at his copy of our murder suspect's photograph told the officer the search was over.

But the case still held one or two more peculiar twists.

In reconstructing the suicide, George and I discovered that the man had climbed a large tree, which was surrounded by mausoleums and tombstones that bore the names of some of Upper Canada's oldest families. He had eased himself out onto a limb that hung directly above a large granite obelisk, which stood about twelve feet tall. After securing the noose around his neck, he lowered himself down until he stood balanced atop the obelisk. Then he jumped. But instead of breaking his neck and dying quickly, he strangled himself in precisely the same slow, cruel manner he had used to kill his wife.

The tombstone from which the man had jumped belonged to a former chief justice of the Supreme Court of Ontario – a rather fearsome jurist who, legend has it, sent no fewer than twelve men to the gallows.

Lying at the foot of his grave marker was the thirteenth.

10

The Scarborough Golf Club Road Murder

In the spring of 1975, when cabby Gord Stoddart was shot to death on a dark, lonely road in the city's east end, enraged taxi drivers from across Toronto ringed Queen's Park in protest, calling for stricter safety measures for their members and the return of the death penalty. For over a week, the case was front-page news, acting as a lightning rod for Torontonians' fear of growing street crime. Though media attention didn't drive this or any other homicide investigation, I and the other members of the squad understood that an early resolution to the case would help to restore the public's confidence in their city and put at ease a lot of very nervous taxi drivers.

"Help! I need help!"

The dispatcher stubs out his cigarette and leans into the mike: "Say again?"

Nothing.

"Come again, that unit. Who's calling? Where are you?"

Straining to hear, he cranks up his speaker and holds one hand aloft to quell the chatter of the phone operators nearby. "Keep it down, will you? One of our guys is in trouble!"

Immediately, they all shut up. Ringing phones go unanswered.

A few seconds pass, then over his speaker there comes a strained, garbled sound he can't quite make out. Then it hits him: the cabby trying to call in is frantically struggling to breathe. He's choking. Somebody asks who it is.

"Don't know. He didn't identify himself or give a location. We'll have to check everybody."

Meanwhile, five miles away in the Metro Police radio room, an officer takes a call from a man who says, "You want to send an ambulance and some cops to Scarborough Golf Club Road at Highland Creek? I just came by there and saw some guy in pretty bad shape. Maybe he cracked up his car or something."

The caller is a truck driver who had been making his way up the dark, isolated section of road that bisects the Scarborough Golf Course when he came upon what looked to him like a car accident. Rather than stop, he drove north to Lawrence Avenue, where he found a phone booth and called in.

While the truck driver is on the line to the police, the taxi dispatcher begins to call each cab in order. Just as he gets to cab 11-43, the last one on his list, one of the phone operators calls to him, "It's the police on the line. They want to know if we've got a cab on Scarborough Golf Club Road."

"Gord Stoddart! I sent him there ten minutes ago to pick up a fare at Masaryktown Hall. When he got there, he asked me what the fare would be to Woodbine and Gerrard."

As he wheels his police cruiser out of the 43 Division parking lot on Lawrence Avenue, Constable Tony Meyler, working the Saturday midnight to Sunday eight a.m. shift, receives a call on his radio.

"Forty-three-o-seven."

"Go ahead."

"Single car P.I., Scarborough Golf Club Road near number four-fifty. Ambulance on the way."

"Forty-three-o-seven, ten-four."

Meyler glances at his watch and scribbles on the clipboard resting on the seat beside him: 12:24 a.m., March 16, 1975.

Speeding west through sparse traffic on Lawrence Avenue East, Meyler wonders how anybody had managed to bang himself up in a car accident on Scarborough Golf Club Road. For days it had been closed to traffic while work crews installed sewers. It was probably somebody who'd gone to a dance at the Masaryktown Hall, which sits on the verge of the ravine overlooking the golf course to the south; somebody with a skinful of booze, no doubt.

Served the bugger right!

Meyler turns off Lawrence and heads south on the road where the accident is reported to have happened, dodging four or five Road Closed signs, until he comes to a dark and lonely stretch, a point one hundred feet south of the single-lane bridge that spans Highland Creek. His headlights pick up a white-and-blue Able Atlantic taxi, number 11-43, angled across the southbound lane and facing south-west with both left-side doors open. A man lies on his back on the roadway, his arms aimlessly thrashing about; they are streaked with blood up to the elbows.

The officer parks his cruiser behind the cab and turns off the engine, positioning the ignition switch so that the cruiser radio remains operational. He winds down the window so he will be able to hear, opens the door, and stands completely still for a moment beside the police car, listening. But all he can hear is water rushing over the rocky creek bed a few feet from the road. Aware that he is now exposed to unseen dangers that may lurk beyond his headlight beams, Meyler fans the surrounding blackness with his flashlight before walking towards the injured man, his eyes squinting into the void, alert for any movement. Always look out for Number One – the unbreakable rule of streetwise coppers everywhere, who understand that if Number One goes down, he's no bloody good to anybody.

As he kneels beside the man, the officer notices that the cab's engine is still running, the headlights are on, and the window in the driver's door is completely shattered. He bends closer to the man's blood-smeared face, trying to detect the odour of alcohol, but there is none. It is then that he notices blood gushing from a small, ragged wound on the left side of the man's neck, near the jaw line. Mere inches away from the man's face, Meyler shouts, "Can you hear me?"

But there is no response, only laboured, uneven breathing.

From his kneeling position beside the prone figure, the officer can see inside the cab a few feet away. There is blood on the steering wheel and on the inside door panel beside the driver's seat. There is also a small pool of blood on the floor beneath the brake pedal. Shiny nuggets of broken glass that were once the driver's window are strewn across the front seat and floor. The hand mike of the taxi radio lies face-down on the driver's seat. It, too, is smeared with blood.

As he kneels on the road taking in the scene, Meyler hears the wail of an ambulance. It arrives seconds later, and he helps the attendants get the man onto the stretcher. As it speeds away, he circles the cab looking for evidence of a collision, but finds none – not on the taxi, the pavement, or the shoulder of the road. He is satisfied that the cab has not been involved in a collision.

Judging from the state of the cab's interior, the shattered window, the small but evil-looking wound on the man's neck, and the isolated location of the taxi, Tony Meyler knows he is dealing with something far more sinister than a personal injury car accident. He walks back to his cruiser and radios for a sergeant to attend the scene, knowing as sure as he's sitting there that sometime, somehow, this matter will end up in a courtroom, and that he'd better be able to give a thorough account of everything he sees and does.

After a moment, the Sergeant responds; he'll arrive in a few minutes. Meyler steps from his cruiser and returns to the cab. Taking the thick piece of yellow crayon he normally uses to chalk the tires of cars for overtime parking, he carefully outlines on the roadway the exact position where the man had lain. That completed, he stands up, turns around and, a half step at a time, walks slowly northward and away from the cab, methodically sweeping the pavement with the beam of his flashlight. At varying intervals of several feet he finds more broken glass and blood. These he carefully circles, and continues to do so until he can find no more. He barely completes this task when he sees the lights of a number of police cars approaching from the north and south. When they are still several hundred feet away, he motions with his hands for them to stop and come no closer, lowering his hands only after he sees the noses of the arriving cruisers dip and slow to a stop across both north and south approaches to the scene, thereby blocking any traffic that might happen along.

From out of the dark, he hears the voice of Sergeant Arvi Tinits: "Whatcha got, Tony?"

Several minutes later, it was evident to Tony Meyler, Arvi Tinits, and my old partner in the Homicide Squad, Jack McBride, that they were dealing with a murder. The cab driver, forty-one-year-old father of two

Gordon Stoddart, didn't make it. He died of a single gunshot wound to the neck soon after his arrival at hospital.

By the time he called me at home to join him at the scene, Jack had been there for a few hours, revving up what would become one of the most intensive and controversial murder investigations of my career. When I got to Scarborough Golf Club Road, here's what we had: a well-liked cab driver and well-loved family man had been gunned down in his taxi at extremely close range, judging from the powder burns on the right side of his neck, and robbery was the likely motive.

That was it. We didn't have a weapon, we didn't have the bullet that had killed Stoddart, because it had gone through his neck from right to left and buried itself somewhere on the golf course across the road from the taxi, and we didn't have any suspects – at least, none whom we could name.

By the time I got to the scene, the cab had already been towed into the garage of 43 Division. It would sit untouched until it was suitable for fingerprinting – a period of a few hours made necessary by the near zero Celsius outdoor temperature and the condensation that would form in and on the cab as soon as it was towed inside the garage. Ident officers wouldn't be able to lift any prints until the cab was completely warm and dry, inside and out.

Cab 11-43 wasn't the only cab in the police garage. A second Able Atlantic taxi, number 11-32, sat beside the one in which Gord Stoddart had been shot. It had been driven that night by a friend of the dead cabby, and was also being dried out and warmed up for fingerprinting.

This other cabby, whom I'll call Tom, had been off the air when Gord Stoddart was dispatched to the Masaryktown Hall. Otherwise, he would have warned his friend not to go there – and for good reason. Moments before, he had dropped three black youths at the front door of the Hall, and they had walked boldly away from his cab without paying him full fare for the ride.

As he sat nervously drinking a coffee in the 43 Division detective office, the cabby gradually began to realize just how close he may have come to taking a bullet himself. He gave us a statement in which he described being flagged down by a black youth at the corner of Lawrence Avenue and Markham Road. The boy asked Tom how much he would charge to drive to Scarborough Golf Club Road. When the cabby told him the fare would be eighty cents, the youth said he'd have to discuss the matter with his two friends, who by that time had already circled the cab. One of them opened the back door and climbed in. The other took a seat in the front beside Tom. Seeing this, the one who'd flagged him down joined the youth in the rear seat.

As Tom headed east along Lawrence, he started the meter. When they got to Scarborough Golf Club Road, he pulled over to the curb and said, "Here you are." The passenger in the front seat said, "There's a club around here we want to go to." Realizing they were probably looking for the Masaryktown Hall, a place he'd only heard of but had never actually seen, Tom made a right turn and headed down the road past the Road Closed and Detour signs. A couple of blocks south, they were met by another Road Closed sign. When Tom told them he could go no further, one of them told him to keep going.

At the top of the hill that descends into the Highland Creek valley, they came upon a barricade.

"I can't drive around this."

"Go around it anyway," ordered the youth sitting beside him in the front seat.

Reluctantly, Tom skirted the barricade and slowly nosed the cab down to the bottom of the valley. Here the road flattened out for several hundred yards, running between eight-foot-high chainlink fences on either side before rising again to the crest of the opposite ravine. At that point, Tom had to drive around a construction trailer that sat in the middle of the road, and then over the CN railway tracks, until he found himself at the edge of a residential area near Dale Avenue.

He stopped the cab and turned on the interior light. From where the cab sat, they could look back across the shallow valley they had just crossed to the lights shining from the windows of what must be the Masaryktown Hall. They could now see that they had unknowingly stopped beside the entrance to the hall when they had paused at the barricade Tom had been ordered to ignore.

"Take us there," said the passenger in the front seat.

The cabby's heart sank. These guys were making him very, very nervous; he just wanted rid of them.

He turned the cab around and headed back up Scarborough Golf Club Road the way they had come, past the construction trailer, along the fence-lined bottom section (faster than he had come, lest they order him to stop there in the dark), and up the hill, where he swung into the laneway of the hall, coming to a stop outside the main entrance. Though lights burned inside, and the place was full of people, neither the outside of the building nor the parking lot were illuminated.

Again, he turned on the interior light. The meter read $1.70. A hand from the rear seat held out a single dollar bill. The cabby took it without a word. Then all three passengers got out, closed the cab doors, and walked towards the building without a backward glance.

Breathing a huge sigh of relief, Tom put the cab in gear and drove away. It was five minutes past midnight. He had two more fares – both lone passengers – before his dispatcher sent him to see the detectives at 43 Division several minutes later. When he pulled into the police station parking lot, he was unaware that Gord Stoddart had been killed.

By early morning, Ident officers had photographed the scene in and around the cab and the surrounding area. In addition, Dave Rigby, one of the best Ident men I've ever worked with, whose reputation for thoroughness was well earned, had dusted both cabs for prints. As even one who is unfamiliar with criminal investigations might imagine, fingerprints on the two taxis were not in short supply. Nevertheless, Rigby dutifully dusted the vehicles, and lifted a number of partial finger and palm prints from both of them.

Over the next few days, with the aid of a magnifying loupe, he would begin the eye-aching task of comparing the prints he lifted from the cabs to fingerprints having similar characteristics and belonging to known criminals. These were stored in RCMP, provincial, and municipal police files across the country. And if no match could be found among those sources, copies of the prints he lifted would be sent to the FBI, in case the person, or persons, who killed Gord Stoddart had ever come to the attention of the American authorities.

The taxis were laden with fingerprints, and somewhere among them were the prints of a murderer, of this Dave Rigby was certain. He was determined to find them, no matter how long it might take.

Before he booked off duty that Sunday, I made one final request of Rigby. I asked him to return to Masaryktown to fingerprint the public pay phone in the lobby on the presumption that one of the three youths Tom dropped off there had used it to call another taxi – Gord Stoddart's.

I'm sure Dave thought it a fruitless exercise to fingerprint a telephone that had probably been handled by many people attending the dance that night. Nevertheless, his professionalism compelled him to comply without complaint. All he said was, "Okeedoke, Bill!" and away he went.

By noon that Sunday, cabbies from Oshawa to Hamilton were aware that one of their number had been gunned down – another victim in a list of crimes against cab drivers that, in recent years, had been growing at an alarming rate. It seemed to them, and with justification, that the criminal element had declared open season on taxi drivers. They were understandably afraid, and from among them came angry calls for the reinstatement of the death penalty.

Of course, the Metro news media jumped all over the story. They covered Gord Stoddart's funeral the following Wednesday, and a benefit hockey game and other fund raisers held for his wife and children in the days that followed. They interviewed angry cab drivers, who were easy to find, sitting as they were behind the wheel of virtually every taxi in the city. Reporters were on hand when the cabbies – five hundred strong – encircled Queen's Park, tying up traffic for a few hours and demanding better safety for their members and minimum sentences for the illegal possession of firearms. They shadowed cabbies as they worked the graveyard shift and wrote gritty, slice-of-life pieces about mean streets, all-night doughnut shops, and drunken, abusive passengers.

While the news media threw every reporter they could spare at the story, we were quietly waging a blitz of our own from the command post we'd established at 43 Division. It is often the practice of homicide investigators to create temporary flying squads of hand-picked police officers from the divisions where murders have occurred. These officers know better than anyone the lay of the land, who to squeeze for information, and what rocks to look under for suspects.

In the Stoddart case, we assembled a team of twenty men who fanned out across 43 and other east Toronto divisions, working their networks of finks and other street people in search of the three black youths suspected of being involved in Stoddart's killing. Jack McBride, Herm Lowe, and I concentrated on criminals with records for armed robbery – especially those known for carrying guns or shaking down cabbies. The investigation was only a few days old when I got a call from a certain high-ranking officer who objected to what he said was my high-handed practice of diverting officers from their usual duties to help with the case.

"With respect, Sir," I said, "I thought we were all on the same police force."

"Be careful, McCormack!" he thundered. "Be very careful, because if you say one more word, *just one*, I'll have your ass for insubordination."

"I'm sorry, Sir," I said, "but I've got a job to do," and promptly hung up on him, fully expecting that once he recovered from the shock of having a subordinate bang a phone down in his ear he'd summon me to Headquarters, do a tap dance up one side of my frame and down the other, then reassign me to the Property Bureau, or to permanent midnights tagging parked cars, or even to walking a beat on the breakwater in front of the Exhibition Grounds. Incredibly, nothing happened. In fact, the silence that emanated from his office was deafening! I heard not a peep – at least not right away. Better still, I got to keep all my men.

By midweek, our team had rousted dozens of rounders with convictions for armed robbery, weapons, and violent assault charges. Those we questioned greeted us with more than the usual amount of resistance and hostility. The suspects in this case were young black men, at least two of whom spoke strongly accented Jamaican patois.

Whenever we cornered a known black bandit to find out where he'd been and what he might know, we got the same song and dance about prejudice and harassment.

"Why you're botherin' me, man? I done notin'."

"We just want to ask you some questions."

"No, man. First you answer me this: Why you're only intress in blacks, man? Why you're not intress in nobody else? Explain me that, man!"

"Turn it down a notch and don't hand me that noise about police harassment! I don't give a shit whether you're black, blue, yellow, or green. I'm talking to you because you've got a sheet for armed robbery, you haven't worked a day since getting out of the joint, and I'll bet if we were to walk back into this dive you've just come out of I'd find half a dozen reasons for your parole officer to yank your ticket! Now, are we gonna talk, or aren't we?"

And so it went.

The day Gord Stoddart was buried, we got a few welcome breaks in the case. A little after noon, Herm Lowe took a call from Dave Rigby:

"Tell Bill I have a match for him on the prints I lifted from the Masaryktown pay phone; they belong to a sixteen-year-old kid by the name of Lloyd Blake."

My long shot had come in!

We checked with Central Records and discovered that a bench warrant had been issued for Blake the previous Friday when he failed to appear in court to answer a theft charge. But we didn't want to scoop him until we found out who he'd been with at Masaryktown.

We found out he lived with his mother in a house near Broadview and Gerrard, and obtained authorization to tap the phone. In the mid-seventies, electronics weren't as advanced as they are today. To conduct a wire tap – "hang a wire" in police parlance – we had to place our recording equipment close to the phone we were tapping. Once again, fortune smiled on us. Almost across the street from Blake's house lived a uniformed sergeant who worked out of 56 Division. Better still, he was already a member of our twenty-man team, and a fine investigator. We hung the wire on Blake's phone, installed the listening and recording equipment in the police officer's house, and assigned him to monitor calls to and from Blake's place twenty-four hours a day. We also installed a portable desk and a typewriter in the officer's house. It was a regular mini–police station out of which our man would work day and night. Perfect! Or so I thought.

As soon as he got wind of what we were doing, the senior officer called me again to demand that I return *his* man to regular uniformed duty, "right bloody now!"

Then and there I decided I'd had a bellyful of this guy's bullshit. Regardless of the consequences, I was prepared to dig in my heels and take whatever punishment came my way. Here was a man who I knew had no idea of how to conduct an investigation, let alone one involving a homicide. He couldn't detect a salami in a wastebasket if his life depended on it, and yet he was telling me what personnel I did and did not need.

I let him have it with both barrels.

"There are some things you'd better understand, Sir! I need this man – *this man!* He's perfectly placed to listen in on these bandits. I've known him for years, and he's a hell of an investigator. He knows every rounder and asshole in the division and where to find them. And he's been a member of our team since we started this investigation.

"And there's something else you'd better understand: You aren't getting him back until we put somebody behind the pipes for this murder!

Go ahead and charge me with insubordination if you're going to, but you are *not* getting him back!"

I figured that by delivering myself of that little homily, I had almost certainly scuttled my career. But at that point, I didn't give a damn. I'd had enough. Here we were, a team of twenty men, working flat out on a major investigation; one of our members was dedicated enough to let us disrupt his entire household and to work round the clock, and this yahoo wanted to yank him off the case and return him to duties that other uniformed sergeants in his division were not only willing, but able, to handle during his absence.

I waited for the explosion, but it never came. Instead:

"Well, *you'd* better understand, McCormack, that if he puts in for even one minute of overtime, I'll nail *both* of you!" *Click!*

I stared incredulously at the phone receiver in my hand. The boys who'd been sitting nearby in our makeshift office at 43 Division, and who had been able to hear only my side of the conversation, sat with mouths agape. I guess they expected to hear me say I'd been summarily suspended, or put on charge, or that I'd have to face some other dire punishment.

But to everyone's relief and surprise, including my own, I suddenly burst out laughing. I laughed so hard, I thought I was going to be sick. This, of course, threw everybody into utter confusion. I'm sure they all thought I was suffering some sort of breakdown. It took a few minutes before I was able to regain my composure long enough to sputter, "Overtime! The stunned sonofabitch was worried about overtime!"

We headed back out on the street and concentrated our efforts on the rounders and punks who hung out in the pool halls and dives around Gerrard Street East. Every so often, we would check back with each other to compare notes. Gradually, we made headway. One kid, and then another, and then a few more, told us that three of their buddies were in hiding because they'd been involved in "something to do with a taxi driver." The names that kept coming up were twenty-year-old Daniel Roosevelt "Boots" Pearce, sixteen-year-old Clarence Christopher "Charlie" Walker, and Lloyd Blake. All of them were known to the police, and they frequented a ramshackle old house on Woodbine Avenue near Gerrard. This was significant because Stoddart had radioed in to ask his dispatcher how much the fare would be from Masaryktown Hall to Woodbine and Gerrard minutes before he transmitted his pitiable plea for help.

That same day, we were contacted by a young woman who told us that while she and her mother were waiting for a bus at the corner of Lawrence Avenue and Markham Road, right about the time Gord Stoddart was shot, they saw three young black men hurry past them. They appeared to be running from something and were extremely agitated. One of them was crying. If she saw these youths again, she could identify them. When we showed her a stack of photos, among which were interspersed pictures of our three suspects, she picked each of them out right away.

Thursday evening, the day after the funeral, Jack McBride and I, along with Detectives Don Madigan and Pat O'Brien, paid a visit to the house on Woodbine Avenue. We encountered a number of young men there who were very surprised, and not altogether happy, to see us. Though we didn't actually end up in a donnybrook with them, we did engage them in discussions about the Stoddart case that might best be described as "candid."

Over the course of a couple of hours, each of them provided us with a written statement that contained pieces of the puzzle – some large, some small. When we assembled them, a very interesting picture began to emerge. It seems that the three young men we sought often came to the Woodbine residence to crash for the night, or to play Jamaican card games and dominoes. At one such get-together, two days before the Stoddart murder, the suspect known as Boots had shown off a loaded revolver and allowed others around the table to handle it. One of the more sensible players got nervous and said he wouldn't play anymore unless Boots put the gun away.

An argument sprang up between Boots and Blake about which store in the area of Woodbine and Gerrard they might rob. While they were arguing, the player who had objected to the presence of the gun unloaded it and tucked it under a pillow. He told us he did so at considerable risk because Boots was known to nurse a fearsome temper. Later in the evening, Boots left for a short time, saying he was going to look for a store to hold up. He returned some time later claiming he had decided not to rob anyone that night.

Saturday evening, Boots, Charlie, and Blake invited one of the Woodbine Avenue residents to join them at a Caribbean party at Masaryktown Hall, but the man declined, saying he'd already been invited somewhere else. He parted company with them at the Woodbine subway station on Danforth Avenue.

By 3:30 Sunday morning, about three hours after Gord Stoddart had been pronounced dead, Boots and Charlie were back at the Woodbine residence, having decided to stay overnight. Blake wasn't with them. He had evidently decided to spend the night at his mother's home not too far away.

It was at noon on Sunday that Boots revealed to one of the occupants of the Woodbine house that his buddy (which one he did not say) had gotten "trigger nervous" and "did something to a taxi driver" when they were at Masaryktown. At first Boots's confidant didn't believe him, and began to laugh. As the day wore on, however, Boots's growing agitation and morbid fascination with news reports of the shooting convinced the other man the story was true.

Another occupant of the Woodbine house gave us a description of the clothing each of the three suspects was wearing when they separated at the subway station Saturday evening. It matched the descriptions given to us by Tom the cab driver and the young woman who saw the three black youths run past her and her mother at the bus stop.

We were told that on the Monday morning following the shooting, and after numerous weekend news reports, which carried descriptions of the youths being sought, Boots borrowed a razor from someone in the Woodbine residence and shaved off his beard and mustache.

We already knew Lloyd Blake was staying at his mother's house (though we didn't let on to these young men that we knew), and when we pressed for the whereabouts of Charlie and Boots, we were told they had fled to Montreal. Where in Montreal nobody in the house knew, but a few of them hinted that a man named Phil just might because he had driven them there the day of Gord Stoddart's funeral.

We left the house on Woodbine Avenue with a half-dozen signed witness statements that, taken together, provided us with a fairly complete picture of what had happened on Scarborough Golf Club Road. We bid the occupants of the house good evening, promising to return if anything they told us — anything at all — didn't check out.

We'd had a long and very productive day, but it wasn't over yet. When we got back to the station, we learned that the officer manning the wiretap had intercepted a phone call placed to Blake's home in Toronto from a hotel in west end Montreal by Boots Pearce. Montreal police had been alerted and had gone to the hotel on Sherbrooke Street West to arrest Pearce, who had rented a room under an assumed name. He had then eluded capture in a scenario worthy of the Keystone Kops.

It seems that the two Montreal detectives who staked out the hotel had decided that their best course of action was to wait for Pearce inside the room; that way, they could put the arm on him as soon as he came through the door. By the time they arrived at the hotel, the two police officers had already put in a long, hard day and were dog tired. After the night manager let them into Pearce's hotel room with his master key, the two weary policemen made themselves as comfortable as they could and sat back in the darkness to wait. Both men were devoted fans of the Montreal Canadiens and decided to kick off their shoes and pass the time by watching the hockey game.

An hour or so after the opening face-off, Pearce returned to the hotel. He unlocked the door to his room and found the two Montreal police detectives glued to the TV set. So intent were they in watching their beloved Habs that they didn't notice him for a minute or two. By the time it dawned on them that their quarry had entered their trap, he was halfway down the hall and headed for the exit. They lumbered after him in their stocking feet. Out the door they ran, across the parking lot and over the grungy late March snowbanks bordering Sherbrooke to Décarie Boulevard, where they lost him – two red-faced, sweating coppers with cold, sore feet and holes in their socks. They missed the rest of the game.

The next day, Herm Lowe flew to Montreal, where he retrieved clothing and other articles that had been seized from Pearce's hotel room. The following Monday morning, the clothing and a stack of photographs that included pictures of all three suspects were shown to Tom, the taxi driver who had dropped the trio off at Masaryktown. He recognized certain articles of clothing as having been worn by two of the suspects and, after thumbing through the mug shots, picked out all three youths who'd been in his taxi.

Monday afternoon, I went to Old City Hall, where I obtained warrants for the arrest of Lloyd Blake, Charlie Walker, and Boots Pearce for the murder of Gord Stoddart. On Wednesday, at about 8:45 a.m., an old blue Chev pulled onto a gas station lot at the corner of Côte-St-Luc Road and Cavendish Boulevard in west end Montreal. Inside were three young black men. One of them got out and pumped eleven dollars' worth of gas into the tank, then hopped back into the car without paying for it. As the car sped away, the gas station attendant ran over to a nearby police car that was stopped at a red light. She told the officers in the cruiser what had happened, and they chased the blue Chev several blocks until the driver lost control and piled into the corner of a house.

Miraculously, no one was hurt. The driver and the passenger who had been sitting in the middle of the front seat of the Chev tried to escape out the driver's door, but were immediately placed under arrest and handcuffed. The passenger on the right side of the car managed to jump from the wreck and lose himself for several hours in the backyards and laneways of the surrounding houses. Eventually, though, the police managed to pick him up. All three were taken to Montreal's Station 14, where they were identified as Godfrey England, the driver of the car, and his passengers, Charlie Walker and Boots Pearce.

At eight that evening, Jack McBride, Herm Lowe, and I were on a plane to Montreal. We were met at the airport by a Montreal police officer who drove us to Station 14. Over the next four hours, we interviewed and took statements from both Walker and Pearce, in which they confessed their part in the killing of Gord Stoddart. Everything they told us fit perfectly with what we had already been able to piece together from the statements of eyewitnesses who saw the youths immediately before and after the shooting, the physical evidence we had gathered at the scene, and what the suspects' friends on Woodbine Avenue had told us about the shooting.

The next day, with Walker and Pearce in our custody, Jack, Herm, and I returned by plane to Toronto, arriving at the airport around suppertime. But we didn't stop to eat. Instead, we all climbed into two waiting police cruisers and began a search for an apartment building that Lloyd Blake was thought to have fled to from his mother's place. Both Walker and Pearce said they could point out the building, located in the northwest corner of the city overlooking Highway 401.

After a couple of hours, we gave up the search for Blake's hideout and began looking for the gun, which Pearce claimed he had thrown among some trees and underbrush not far from the taxi. While Jack McBride accompanied other officers to the golf course, Pearce was driven there by the first officer to have arrived at the scene of the shooting a week and a half before, Tony Meyler, a fellow Jamaican in whom Boots Pearce had begun to show some trust.

Leaving the police cruisers behind them on Scarborough Golf Club Road, Pearce and the police officers began to retrace the route he, Walker, and Blake had taken through the western section of the golf course in the direction of Markham Road. As they walked, Pearce whispered to Meyler, "If them find the gun, them a go charge me with it, and for carry it cross the border?"

Jack cast an inquiring glance at Tony, who repeated Pearce's question. Together, Jack and Tony assured Pearce that the murder charge would be the only one he would face.

Pearce seemed to consider their response for a moment, then said, "Shine your light over there." He pointed to a wooded area, and said, "I was running by here, and stopped and flung it wit' all my might into the bushes because I didn't want nobody to find it."

Jack and three uniformed men began searching the area Pearce had pointed out. After several minutes, they still hadn't come up with the gun, and Pearce, who wasn't dressed for winter, began complaining of the cold. Jack instructed Meyler to take him back to the cruiser so he could get warm.

On the way back to the police car, Pearce became talkative, asking what Meyler thought would happen to him in court, how long his sentence might be, where he might be sent to prison. He also asked Tony how long he'd been in Canada, and what town he came from in Jamaica. Tony answered all of Pearce's questions honestly. By the time they got back to the cruiser, Pearce was in a melancholy mood, saying he was afraid to go to prison, and that he longed to return to Jamaica.

"Boy, I want go home, now. If I was home, this would not happen."

He gave Tony a sorrowful and self-pitying account of his life since coming to Canada, saying he was the last child born into his family, and that he'd brought shame to his brothers and sisters. He told the officer he had stolen the gun from his uncle's place in Michigan, and that he hoped his uncle wouldn't get into any trouble on his account. Then he looked directly into Tony's eyes and asked, "Do you know how it happened?"

Meyler: "No, but you don't have to tell me anything unless you want to."

Pearce: "Well, I will anyway. Me and Lloyd and Charlie went to some dances at Masaryktown Hall and everybody used to take guns and fire them in the air and make a lot of noise. And that weekend, I decide to take mine to fire in the air, like everybody else.

"We took the bus to Markham and Lawrence and waited for a while, and didn't see no bus coming along, so we flagged down a taxi, and I sat in the back because I had the gun till we got to Masaryktown Hall.

"When we got there, the taxi fare was $1.70, and we gave the taximan a dollar. And while the three of us was putting together the seventy cents, because we did not have a lot of money, just some change, the taximan drove away.

"When we went to the Hall, we saw it was some white people dance, so Lloyd went in and use the phone to call another taxi so we could go to Eglinton to catch a bus to go home.

"While we were waiting, Charlie asked me for the gun, and I gave it to him. When the taxi come, Charlie got in the back because he had the gun, and I was in front. The driver turn on the meter and it was sixty cents, and I ask him how much to Gerrard and Woodbine, and he said five dollars and something. I tell him to stop and let us out because I know we did not have enough money. And he wouldn't stop, and we were afraid he would call the police when we told him we did not have the money, and the police would find the gun. So Charlie put the gun to the taximan's head and tell him must stop. And then I hear a *bang!* and I say, 'Charlie!' And we jump out and Charlie give me back the gun and we run across the golf course and I hide the gun because we were scared, and Lloyd was crying."

Pearce spoke slowly and deliberately in the same Jamaican patois Tony Meyler had grown up with, allowing the officer to write down every word he said. He paused for a minute, evidently considering something. Then: "If I tell you where the gun is, will you tell them?"

Tony told him he must.

"I will tell you anyway. But I am not telling them. You can show them."

"You know, Boots, they've been out there for quite a while. When they find out they've been looking in the wrong place, they aren't going to be very happy."

"Just tell them I made a mistake. It's over on Markham Road, near the fence. I'll show you. I would not lie to you. Blow the horn and call them."

"If I blow the horn, they might think something happened and come running."

"What you mean? Them might think that me escape, or do you something? Them know me now. So why am I going to escape for?"

Pearce broke into a laugh and kept insisting that Meyler blow the cruiser horn to summon Jack and the others. Just as Tony had predicted, the men came running. But he waved to them as they approached to signify that all was well — even if he was about to tell them they had been slogging through mud and the remnants of that winter's snow, freezing their butts off, in search of a gun that wasn't there. Pearce guided the officers to a place on Markham Road where the gun was eventually found beside a hydro pole.

The arrest of Walker and Pearce soon hit the news, and kept the pressure on us to find Lloyd Blake. Word on the street was he had gone to ground somewhere in Toronto's west end. We would not know until a few days had elapsed that a member of Toronto's West Indian community had befriended the boy and, knowing the police were looking for him, had tried to convince Blake to turn himself in. He was afraid that if he tried to force the boy to give himself up, he'd run, and forever be lost. So he patiently listened, then encouraged, then listened some more. His was likely the first voice of reason Blake had heard in many a day. But it would be a few days more before the boy could summon sufficient courage to take the man's advice.

It's a hard, cold fact of life on the police force that cadets — uniformed civilians under the age of twenty-one who hope to be police officers one day — occupy the lowest rung on the ladder. They are everybody's gopher, and those who occupy the rungs above them – including the station cleaning staff – consider it their sworn duty to verbally smack down all cadets lest their youthful heads become too big for their shoulders. They are treated like cubs in a wolf pack who must endure the corrective snarls and cuffs of every adult member of the group until they reach maturity.

Twenty-year-old David Theriault was just such a cub on March 31, 1975, when, at about 11:30 p.m., a slender black youth dressed in a clean white shirt and a dark blue suit walked nervously up to him as he stood behind the bustling front counter of Metro's 31 Division on Sheppard Avenue West.

"I believe you're looking for me."

The cadet could hardly hear him above the routine commotion around him.

"What do you mean?" he asked.

Blake pointed to a photo of himself on a poster on the bulletin board near the front counter and said, "That's me up there."

Cadet Theriault looked at Lloyd Blake's picture on the poster and back at Blake, then, barely able to conceal his excitement, said, "Come this way," opening a swinging gate to allow Blake to walk behind the counter, where Theriault placed his hand on the boy's shoulder. Unsure of what to do next, the young cadet looked questioningly to Constable Fred Lamorandiére, who happened to be standing nearby.

"What you got, kid?"

Somewhat surprised, and not a little self-conscious, Theriault said simply, "A guy for murder."

Around them heads swivelled, conversations ceased, and, for an instant, everyone appeared to be frozen to the spot. Then, before Cadet Theriault knew it, his first big pinch was taken from him. Blake was trundled off to the detective office by a couple of uniformed men, who wasted no time in calling the Homicide Squad.

Just as Walker and Pearce had done before him, Lloyd Blake gave us a full confession.

All three youths were held in custody pending a preliminary hearing that was set for August. In June, a major controversy erupted when Blake was released temporarily from custody. His mother had posted bail on his behalf, but withdrew it when she saw the storm of protest that greeted her son's release – mostly from irate cabbies who, once again, encircled the parliament buildings at Queen's Park, calling for stricter bail laws.

Eventually, there was a trial. When it was over, the jury deliberated for a relatively short time before convicting Charlie Walker of manslaughter, not murder, and acquitting Boots Pearce and Lloyd Blake.

Walker was sentenced to five years in a federal penitentiary, and deported to Jamaica upon his release. In 1997, he was arrested in Toronto for re-entering Canada illegally. That same year, had he lived, Gord Stoddart would have been sixty-three years old.

11

"The Deputy Wants to See You"

It had never occurred to me that I might one day be transferred out of Homicide, but one drizzly fall morning in 1979 it happened and I was taken completely by surprise. I must confess that I didn't welcome the transfer. I wanted to protest that there'd been a foul-up. Then I tried to convince myself it was just a matter of time before I'd be back. But – thank goodness – I was wrong.

Sandra Morgan walked across the Homicide Squad office to the desk, where I sat typing a report.

"Inspector Sellar wants to see you, Bill."

There was something in her tone that told me there was nothing routine about Sellar's summons. One look at Sandra's face told me I was right. But I knew better than to ask her for an explanation. It would have forced her to make up a story, and that would have embarrassed us both. Sandra was too good a friend for that. She is a person who can be relied upon to keep a confidence. And as the only civilian member of the Homicide Squad, responsible for typing up the voluminous crown briefs every team of detectives lugged into court, she had been entrusted with many a secret.

"Where is he?" I asked.

"In his office."

George Sellar proved to be as inscrutable as Sandra had been.

"You wanted to see me, Inspector?"

"Actually, it's Deputy Noble who wants to have a word with you, Bill."

"What's it about, sir?"

"He told me you should go right up," said Sellar, ignoring my question and busying himself with paperwork.

I tormented myself with questions as I walked through Headquarters towards Deputy Chief Jim Noble's office. What had I done? Was I on somebody's shit list? I had no enemies that I could think of — at least none who could do me any harm on the job. My clearance record was pretty good: over one hundred homicide cases in ten years and only one unsolved. I racked my brain as I stood outside Noble's office, but couldn't come up with a single plausible answer as to why the deputy wanted to see me.

"Come in," he said. "Close the door and sit down."

When I saw my personnel file open on his desk, I knew this was serious. Noble didn't waste any time getting to the point.

"It's time for a change, Bill. Don't you think?"

"A change, sir?"

"Well," he said, thumbing through my file, "you've been on the job twenty years — four in uniform, six in plainclothes, and the last ten in Homicide. Time to move on, wouldn't you say?"

I was dumbfounded. Why should I want to transfer out of the squad? In my mind, homicide detectives were the epitome of the police investigator. It was the most fulfilling work I'd ever done. "Have I screwed up somewhere along the line, sir?" I stammered in disbelief.

"Screwed up?" he asked.

I'd really meant it as a rhetorical question, but Noble seemed to actually consider the possibility seriously for a moment. Or so I thought until I detected the slightest hint of a smile playing on his lips.

"No, Bill. Nothing like that. It's just that we have plans for you. The department wants to add a little polish to the old man, so to speak."

Over the course of the next fifteen minutes it was clear that the deputy's mind was made up. He said that when my tour of duty ended that day, so would my ten-year stint in Homicide. At that moment I felt a deep, dull ache as though I'd lost a limb. What was I going to say to the other members of the squad? What was I going to tell Jean? I'd given everything I had to this job and now I was being shipped out. It didn't seem fair.

It was hard for me to walk back into the Homicide office. But while I was up talking to the deputy, George Sellar had made saying good-bye much easier for me by gathering together those who were on duty that day and telling them that I'd be moving on. By the time I got back downstairs, everybody knew. Sandra had even called the guys who were off duty to let them know. I went from one to the other shaking hands and receiving everyone's good wishes. The last person I said good-bye to was my dear friend and longtime partner, Herm Lowe. We had been through so much together. Herm was the limb whose loss I had already begun to mourn.

"This move is going to be good for you, Bill, I know it," he assured me.

Deputy Noble had ordered me to report to the inspector in charge of 32 Division on Yonge Street bright and early the following Monday – "in harness," as police call wearing the uniform. I hadn't worn blue serge since 1962, so it meant a trip to the quartermaster for boots and a new uniform, complete with a staff sergeant's crowns and chevrons (the equivalent rank in uniform to a detective sergeant).

Pressed and polished and feeling awkward as hell in my new uniform, I walked through the front door of 32 Division at six o'clock Monday morning. To my surprise and delight, I was greeted by Fred Lock, who used to work out of the Auto Squad, which had occupied the office next door to mine at Headquarters. Fred had been transferred to 32 some months before. I was happy to learn that he'd be my station duty officer. As I walked behind the front counter, he handed me a steaming cup of coffee.

"Double cream, double sugar, right?"

"Bless you, my son!"

"Only the first one of the day's on me, Bill."

Despite the warm welcome I received from Fred and so many others at 32 Division, I knew it was not going to be easy to adjust to life as a divisional staff sergeant. On afternoon and midnight shifts, I would be the ranking officer in the station, responsible for upwards of fifty police officers, as well as whomever they happened to lock up in the cells. While it is an extremely important job, it is one that is done from behind a desk, and it seldom involves direct contact with the kind of carnage that had for a decade been my stock-in-trade. I would need a way to separate myself from those years of exposure to human tragedy and violence. Soon I began to tally my experiences on the squad, and in doing so I would come to terms with the psychological and emotional costs I had incurred.

Jean was very supportive. She knew how much I would miss the squad. But she also must have known it was time for me to break new ground.

"Bill, you've come a long way from the days when you walked a beat. When the department moved you out of uniform and into the detective office, you were excited, but you were also upset at the thought of leaving your buddies behind. You felt the same way when you were transferred to Homicide. Every change – even a good one – is upsetting. Take this in your stride. Besides, I know they're grooming you. Mark my words."

Jean has always called things the way she saw them. For forty years, she's been my rock. More than any other person, Jean understood the deep, unspoken anguish I often felt for homicide victims and their families, especially when the victim was a child. Indeed, one such case was almost more than I could bear. It involved the battering death of a tiny soul named Elizabeth, whose two-year-old body had been so thoroughly and savagely pummelled by her mother's boyfriend that Dr. Margaret Norman, the excellent pathologist who performed the postmortem, had difficulty finding a single unbroken bone in that pathetic little corpse.

During the autopsy, I was unable to banish from my mind images of my own two daughters, Kathy and Lisa, or to fathom how anyone could have so badly abused such an angel. Dr. Norman must have sensed my emotional turmoil, and to my everlasting gratitude, she waited until I got a grip on myself before resuming her very necessary work, which, I'm glad to say, helped us get a conviction.

That night, I booked off duty and took the long way home. After an hour or so, I turned slowly up our street, pulled into the driveway, and turned off the car's engine. For several minutes I sat alone in the dark, unable to go into the house. Eventually I did go in. Everybody had gone to bed, so I tiptoed down the hall and into our daughters' bedroom. Eleven-year-old Kathy and six-year-old Lisa were safely tucked up in their bunk beds, fast asleep. For a long time, I leaned against the doorjamb and watched the shallow rise and fall of their little tummies. I kissed each of them gently on the forehead, then hurried from the room before the sobs that had been welling up inside me could erupt.

Little Elizabeth was among five child homicide victims I would have to deal with that year alone. It was one aspect of the job that I would not miss.

For their part, my family appeared to welcome the change because it meant my work schedule would be predictable, and I could now be depended upon to attend our kids' birthday parties and to be at home the odd Christmas morning. I'd spent many a Christmas Day bent over a corpse while my children opened their gifts or helped their mother set the dining room table for a turkey dinner I'd only get to pick at hours later, after trudging home weary with the stench of death in my nostrils and on my clothing. Though none of them has ever called me to account, I know my frequent absences from important family times took their toll on Jean and the kids. I seldom let on, but it used to tear me up, too.

In time, I began to understand that the years I'd spent on the Homicide Squad had been more valuable than I had previously supposed. For one thing, they provided me with unique insights into human behaviour. And as I began to rise through the senior ranks on my way to becoming Chief of the Metropolitan Toronto Police, I realized just how well my homicide work, together with my experiences from working in numerous other branches of the police service, had equipped me to deal with the host of problems that come with the job of running a major urban police department.

But that's another story.